MOUNTAIN BIKING NORTH

For my Dad, Charles William Dennis Mitchell, born in 1920, who rode and raced a Reynolds 531 framed, fixed-wheel single speed, and saw his first mountain bikers riding the jungle trails of Burma in WW II. He still rides his mountain bike.

MOUNTAIN BIKING NORTH
34 GREAT RIDES IN NEW ZEALAND'S NORTH ISLAND

Text and photographs by Dave Mitchell
Maps by Geographx

craig potton publishing

First published in 2011 by Craig Potton Publishing

Craig Potton Publishing
98 Vickerman Street, PO Box 555, Nelson, New Zealand
www.craigpotton.co.nz

© Maps by Geographx

© Photography and text: Dave Mitchell

ISBN: 978 1 877517 49 5

Printed in China by Midas Printing International Ltd

A wild sky on the Old Coast Road, near Wellington

ACKNOWLEDGEMENTS

Firstly, I want to acknowledge those enlightened members of the Department of Conservation who see mountain biking as a legitimate recreation in our national parks, forest parks, recreation reserves and the vast public lands we all own. They have built new tracks and upgraded old ones for us to enjoy.

I would also like to acknowledge the New Zealand Cycleway Project, which has already created some great cycle trails and will eventually add hundreds of kilometres of riding to the national trail network. Thanks to all the local volunteers, councils and clubs who have raised funds and participated in track building and maintenance around the country. I also want to thank the Ground Effect crew for creating a track-building slush fund and for providing encouragement and advice.

Special thanks go to my partner Ditte van der Meulen, who not only keeps me organised and on track, but has taken many of the images in this book, while Stephanie Turner provided her language skills to help with the writing. Thanks to Sue and Jaap van Dorsser, Jonathan Kennett, Mike Pearce, Kevin and Jenny Loe, Carl Patton, Karl Ratahi and John Carman, and finally to all those farmers and land owners who allow access into their special piece of New Zealand.

Forgive me for any errors, omissions and misdirections, and please inform the publisher so that corrections can be made to future editions.

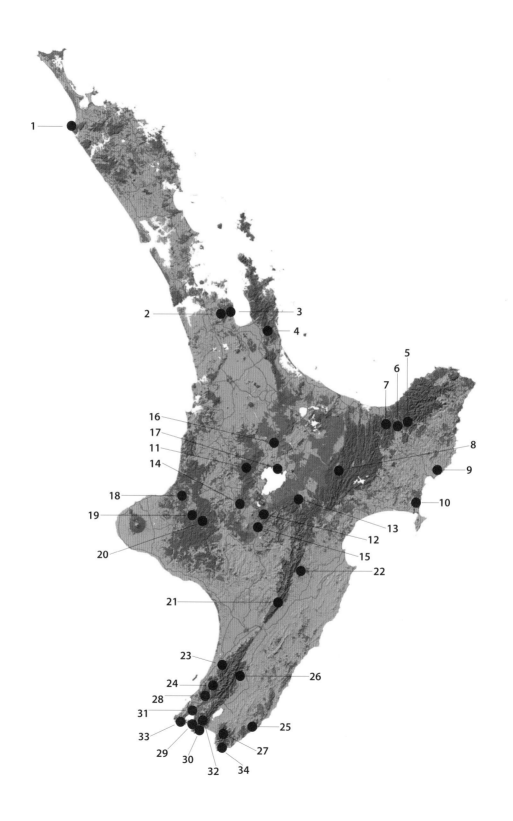

CONTENTS

INTRODUCTION

The North Island is a great place to mountain bike. Primeval jungle covers much of its squat mountain ranges, with tall podocarps towering above the lower canopy, and a huge variety of ferns and broadleaves along the tracks and trails. The warm climate and regular rainfall sustain plants and birds found nowhere else on the planet. The rugged beauty of the coastline contrasts with open farmland in the east and west, while the massive volcanoes of Tongariro and Egmont national parks dominate the central region. Geothermal activity has created the lakes around Taupo and Rotorua, along with hot pools, springs and geysers. North of Auckland lies kauri country and the winterless Tai Tokerau, where miles of sandy beaches stretch to the very tip of New Zealand.

In the mid 1980s mountain bikes became yet another piece of recreational equipment introduced to New Zealand. Many of the early bikes, resplendent with carriers and pannier bags, were lugged over by American tourists and merely used to cycle-tour New Zealand, based on a perception that we had a rough and ready second-world roading system. Instead they found a network of roads more suited to European touring bicycles or cyclocross mounts. When their owners left the country, most of these bikes were traded or sold into the hands of Kiwis looking for a faster and more efficient way into the back country.

This was by no means the first time pioneering Kiwis had used fat-tyred bicycles in the backblocks of New Zealand. Indeed there are stories of adventurous cyclists piloting penny-farthings on little more than goat tracks along the South Island's wild and rugged West Coast in the late 1800s. The many cycling clubs that thrived around the turn of the nineteenth century had a history of epic trips on rugged tracks and trails, which at the time made up much of the country's roading network.

The specialised mountain bike provided a strong frame of chromoly steel and a group of components that could take the rough and tumble of off-road riding. They could climb steep hills and descend them without the fear of brake fade or failure, broken forks or bent frames—a perfect recipe for long distance trips into the unknown with the possibility of returning in one piece.

They have evolved rapidly to become lighter, stronger, suspended and more accessible to the average rider. They float along riverbeds, swoon sweet single track, descend huge mountains and climb some of the steepest tracks you could imagine. But let's not forget it takes a rider to push things along, and many of us rose to the challenge and still keep it going to this day.

Alexei Sayle once said 'They are the most efficient form of movement on the surface of the planet', and I guess he's got a point. In fact some experts say it is the most efficient machine ever invented, returning a calorific equivalent of 3000 miles per gallon, in automotive terms. They are a stand up, sit down, walking, running and tramping machine. Hopefully this book will inspire you to turn the pedals and explore New Zealand on your mountain bike, whether it be local tracks or far-flung ones in the remotest part of the high country. Their magical ability to amplify one's physical efforts still amazes me after all these years.

Length and Difficulty

A few of the rides in this book are downright hard and gnarly, requiring a high level of skill and fitness, but most are well within the realms of the average rider. Even the hard ones can be broken down into manageable chunks so you can still enjoy them. They will build stamina and moral fibre, expand your horizons and hopefully help you appreciate what a wonderful place and time we live in.

Weather is the most important factor to consider for any trip, and New Zealand seems to have very variable weather at any time of year. The cornerstone of any ride is to book fine weather with light winds, maybe even a tail wind for the returning leg. River crossings can be just as dangerous for mountain bikers as they are for trampers; soft snow will stop you dead, and strong winds can sometimes make riding impossible, especially on the tops.

Maps and Navigation

The Department of Conservation (DOC) as well as regional and local councils produce some excellent pamphlets on mountain biking areas. From my experience they provide good general information but you will still need a New Zealand topo map to navigate your way in detail. This is especially important in the back country, as pre-ride planning with topo maps can give you a good indication of the terrain, river crossings, alternate tracks and expected distance and climbing. I take a GPS and compass, and am regularly surprised that where I thought I was on the map was not where the GPS indicated. A GPS can get you out of trouble when the clouds roll in, but remember, it is electronic and can fail at the drop of a hat.

Huts

New Zealand's hut network is ideal for overnight mountain bike trips. Without huts, the tents, sleeping mats and extra paraphernalia required for a night out make biking so much harder and less accessible. To arrive at a hut with a lightweight sleeping bag and extra food is pure pleasure in comparison, and opens up all sorts of riding possibilities. Treat huts as if you own them, and make room for others as if they own them. Carry out all your rubbish and leave them as you would like to find them. Buy the appropriate hut tickets and expect to pay for private huts.

Water, Footprint and Responsibility

Most New Zealand streams and rivers provide safe drinking water, just avoid those in farm country that don't come from a bush gully or the high tops. When doing a tops trip carry adequate water and pre-plan for the fill up points along the way using your topo map. Leave only tyre tracks, and take only air, water, memories and digital images. Ask permission to ride on private land. Most landowners are more than willing to share their back country if it doesn't interfere with their day to day farming. Leave all gates as you find them and don't run stock.

Safety and Equipment

The key to survival and having a great trip is firstly preparation, followed by fitness and equipment. Your body, like your bike, should be well maintained and fit for the purpose. The ride should be planned and the weather gods and oracles consulted, and their predictions duly noted and acted upon. Gear taken should match the conditions and expected terrain. Plans B, C and D will give you alternative options to head for the best weather and riding conditions with less pressure and more pleasure. Pick your riding buddies accordingly. Have fun and ride hard, but don't be shy about turning back if conditions make it necessary.

Grading

1 Flat and relatively smooth, suitable for those starting out.
2 Mainly flat, with short gradual climbs that require some fitness and skill.
3 More challenging climbs and terrain requiring a medium level of fitness and skill.
4 Challenging climbs, descents and technical riding requiring a good level of skill and fitness. May involve some bike carrying.
5 Gnarly and long climbs with challenging descents and technical riding requiring a high level of skill and fitness. Some bike carrying required.

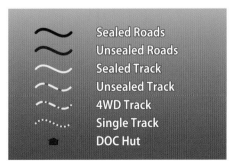

	Sealed Roads
	Unsealed Roads
	Sealed Track
	Unsealed Track
	4WD Track
	Single Track
	DOC Hut

TAUROA PENINSULA TRAIL
NORTHLAND

Fourteen kilometres west of Kaitaia at the southern end of Ninety Mile Beach sits the town of Ahipara, the surf-casting capital of New Zealand, which has a long history of Maori settlement. Ahipara means 'Sacred Fire' and is in the tribal area of the Te Rarawa people, who are descendants of the people who migrated across the Pacific in the waka Tinana. By the late 1800s the town had over 1000 residents, mainly Dalmatian immigrants who were attracted by the kauri gum fields and the high price gum fetched for commercial varnishes and linoleum.

The Tauroa Peninsula Trail, also known as the Tutu Trail or Crunchy Trail, circumnavigates the Tauroa Peninsula, but the coastal section can only be ridden three hours either side of low tide. The ride starts from Ahipara and crosses Wairoa Stream on Foreshore Road, heading west around the long curve of Ahipara Bay. You then climb steeply and cross Pukerua Creek continuing up to a Y intersection. Take the left track onto the metalled Gumfields Road (which may not be signposted) and climb up into the gum fields. There are excellent views north up the long stretch of Ninety Mile Beach to Cape Reinga.

Continue down this well-worn gravel road for a few kilometres to a large corrugated iron building and a gum field museum. This is all that remains of a once thriving community, at one time numbering over a thousand gum diggers, who supported three hotels and a number of shops. Check out the museum and ask about the beach access and track condition.

The track starts just after these buildings and wanders west over a wide 200-metre-high plateau of stunted manuka to the sea. It's a very rough, rocky and sandy 4WD track that has weathered down to bedrock for most of the way. After 3 kilometres a short side track climbs north to a strategic lookout with commanding views across the extensive sand hills to the coast. Green pockets of regenerating native bush thrive along the streamways, contrasting with the white sand.

The main track now climbs steeply next to a row of gnarly old-man pine trees to the edge of the dunes. From the end of the track a rocky outcrop overlooks the descent down the face of a dune to a long line of waves breaking along the beach. Find a route between the Waitaha and Tanutanu streams, but aim for the more northerly Tanutanu Stream mouth. There is usually a set of quad bike tracks to follow.

Push or carry your bike down the dunes if the integrity and long life of your drive train is important to you. If you have the tides right, the lower section is rideable on the hard-packed sand of the beach, and with a bit of luck the prevailing wind will help push you up the coast. Beyond Okura Creek rocky outcrops extend as shallow shelves into the sea, with the outgoing tide leaving many colourful rock pools behind.

Lighthouse 62 is perched on a limestone bluff just before the first of dozens of baches comes into view. Some of these are the original huts that have served generations of seaweed pickers, who collected agar seaweed from the rocks and kauri gum washed up by the sea. There are some short sections where you may have to push your way through the soft sand as you head for Tauroa Point, where Ninety Mile Beach and Ahipara come back into view. The rocky outcrops continue to Shipwreck Bay, where one of its victims is still visible at low tide. From the bay continue around Te Angaanga Beach and carry your bike over a large rocky outcrop at its eastern point. On the far side you can ride the lower end of Ninety Mile Beach back to the Ahipara township. They have great ice creams at the dairy and there's a good motor camp at the north end of town.

On the edge of the dunes before the sandy descent to the beach

Encountering the first of the Peninsula's baches

Map: AV25 Tauroa Peninsula
Distance: 35 km
Climbing: 350 metres
Grade: 2–3
Notes: Check tide tables as the coastal section can only be ridden three hours either side of low tide.

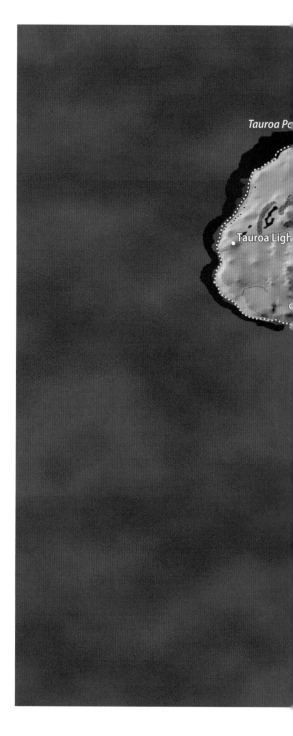

Tauroa Po

Tauroa Ligh

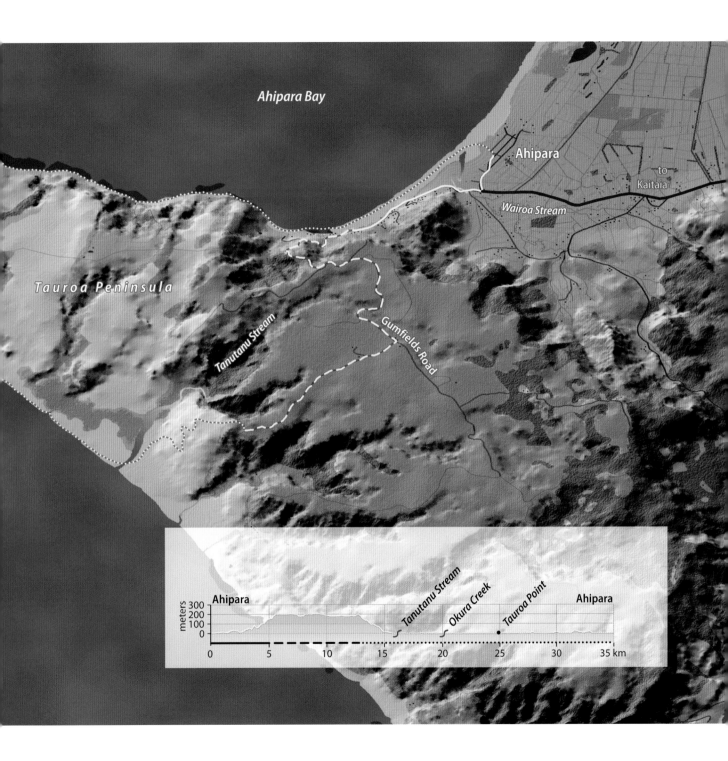

Ahipara Bay

Ahipara

to Kaitaia

Wairoa Stream

Tauroa Peninsula

Tanutanu Stream

Gumfields Road

meters
300
200
100
0

Ahipara

Tanutanu Stream

Okura Creek

Tauroa Point

Ahipara

0   5   10   15   20   25   30   35 km

MANGATAWHIRI–MOUMOUKAI TRACKS
HUNUA RANGES

Five large reservoirs and dams have been built in the Hunua Ranges, with another five in the Waitakere Ranges west of Auckland. Together they form an integral part of the greater Auckland water supply network. Their vast catchments were initially set aside to preserve water quality, but soon became important recreational reserves. The first were built in the early 1960s, with additions and improvements added as Auckland water demands increased.

Circling around the Upper Mangatawhiri Campground are the Mangatawhiri Challenge Track, the Mangatawhiri River Track and the Moumoukai Farm Track. They can be easily connected to form a challenging day ride. To get there, head to Hunua, which is approximately 10 kilometres south of Clevedon or 11 kilometres east of Papakura City. Turn east off Hunua Road 5 kilometres south of Hunua onto Moumoukai Road. This narrow sealed road soon turns to gravel and climbs to the park entrance. Descend carefully to the Upper Mangatawhiri Campground. This is an excellent spot below the dam, with the campsite in a large, open paddock edged by a stream and tall, shady manuka trees.

Start the Mangatawhiri Challenge Track by riding north up Waterline Road to the dam, then climb up to the reservoir and round its perforated edge to the far end. Regenerating bush growing down to the water makes it appear like a natural lake, and the track around the shore is shady and cool. At the end of the reservoir, climb to a Y intersection and go left onto Wairoa Hill Road. This area was once extensively logged, and still sports pine plantations on its western slopes. After about 500 metres, select granny gear and hang a left up an old skidder track next to an MTB marker.

This piece of single track climbs very steeply to the 370-metre ridge top and provides a panoramic view across the Hunua Ranges and west to the Wairoa Reservoir. It's a pretty gnarly grade 4 track that undulates along the ridge, offering up some awesome and often slippery descents on slick clay. Much of the surrounding bush has regenerated above the view line as the track travels south to a basic shelter and lookout. The final descent is a fast pylon road that plummets down to Repeater Road.

Turn left on Repeater Road, and at the Moumoukai Road intersection head back towards camp through the park entrance. Ride down the hill for about a kilometre to turn left again at an MTB marker onto an amazingly tight but short section of single track that links back up with the road at the bottom of the hill. Head towards camp and take the first right onto a major gravel road. Follow this road south for a kilometre, then go left at the River Track sign. This superb piece of single track flows through mixed bush to join Manning Road. Head left and then right onto Mangatangi Hill Road for a short distance. Red MTB markers direct you to the right and back onto the single track of the Moumoukai Farm Track.

Slicing through the regen on River Track

Wairoa Hill Road

Waterline Road

Upper Mangatawhiri
Reservoir

HUNUA RANGES

Wairoa Reservoir

Moumoukai

Repeater Road

Moumoukai Road

Mangatawhiri River

to
Hunua

to
Ramarama

Moumoukai

Repeater
Road

Moumoukai

Moumoukai

meters

400

200

0

Waterline Rd

Mangatawhiri River

0   5   10   15   20   25   30   35 km

Steep slippery ridge top section between the Wairoa and Mangatawhiri Reservoirs

This is a mix of open country and old farm tracks joined by sweet single track that wind their way south through beautiful bush and then loop around to return on Moumoukai Road and Mangatangi Hill Road back to camp. There are some cool river crossings, steep climbs and gnarly descents thrown into the mix, with a fantastic variety of scenery to enjoy. A few old kauri trees and some young ones can be spotted from the track, with rimu, totara and kahikatea also pointing skywards. These are the sort of tracks that make you want to stay the night and do it all over again the next day.

Maps: BB33 Hunua, Auckland Regional Council Hunua Park Map
Distance: 35 km
Climbing: 850 metres
Grade: 4 & 2+
Notes: The official park map is the best one to navigate by (http://www.arc.govt.nz/parks/our-parks/parks-in-the-region/hunua-ranges/). To camp, contact the ARC Parks Dept by phone on 09 366 2000. The Challenge Track is not recommended in the wet.

WAHARAU RIDGE TRACK
FIRTH OF THAMES

The land that eventually became Waharau Regional Park was originally purchased in the early 1970s by the Auckland Regional Authority to provide access to the water catchments that stretch from the Firth of Thames into the eastern foothills of the Hunua Ranges. Maori first arrived in the 14th century, with Ngati Whanaunga occupying the land from the 17th century. The coast became the summer residence for the Maori king from the 1890s, and Tainui still maintain a campground in the park.

From the 1860s vast tracts of kauri and beech were logged and shipped to Auckland and the Coromandel mining towns. The lower slopes of the Hunua Ranges were eventually cleared and are still farmed today. Appropriately, the Maori queen opened the park in 1979.

The park entrance is 38 kilometres south of Clevedon and 9 kilometres north of Kaiaua on East Coast Road, which runs along the edge of the Firth of Thames. Blackberry Flat Campsite and picnic area is the perfect place to start the ride from, only a few hundred metres off East Coast Road.

From the camp, follow the red-, yellow- and blue-topped marker pegs northwest up the hill. This old farm track heads through a few sheep paddocks and into bush. Tall kanuka line the narrowing track as it climbs steeply and heads up the Waharau Ridge. Select granny gear for this single track climb, which affords excellent grip on the well-draining leaf-litter surface. The regenerating forest is lush and green, full of ferns, broadleaves and hard beech. Tawa, rimu, rata and totara are also re-emerging in favourable spots. The Lower Link Track (blue, 4 km) peels off less than a kilometre up the ridge with the Upper Link (yellow, 5.8 km) peeling

View from the Ridge Track of the Firth of Thames and the Coromandel Ranges

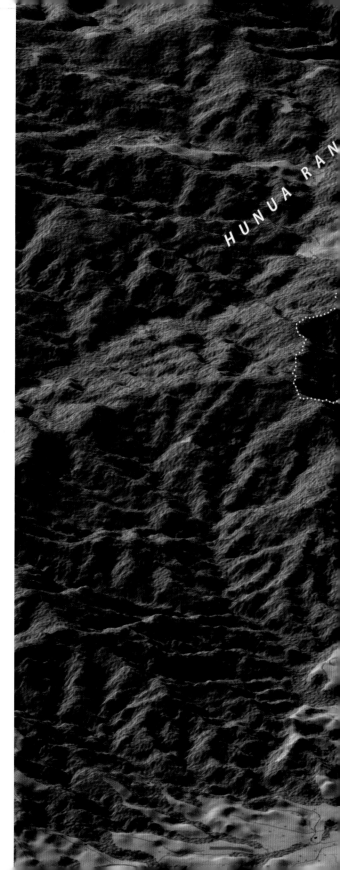

off a kilometre further on. Both loop back around to camp and are ideal for those wanting just a short spin.

The red markers continue to a T intersection where an old forestry road is reached at the very top of the climb. The Waharau Ridge Track swings left and you ride south downhill through a tunnel of forest to the second T intersection. Ignore the red markers and pedal along the single track that traverses mainly uphill through a damp, dense forest. This is the southern section of the Waharau Ridge Track and has some great technical riding thrown in. At the third T intersection hang a left and head to the east coast on a well-formed forestry road. This is now the Whakatiwai Track, which runs through an extensive regenerating forest before emerging into farmland with stunning views across the Firth of Thames to the Coromandel Peninsula. It's a fast, and in places rough, downhill, with a few gates to shut behind you on the way to the sea.

The track ends at the East Coast Road carpark with a couple of ride options to consider. Head north up the coast for 5 kilometres and back to the main park entrance, or better still ride back up the gnarly, steep Whakatiwai Track. You can then revisit the superb single track section of the Waharau Track back to the second T intersection, but this time in a downhill direction. Go right and follow the red track markers towards the Blackberry Campsite. The track plunges down a narrow bench between tall kanuka on hard clay and fine scree. It seems to go on forever until a final river crossing, then a farm track emerges and takes you back out to Blackberry Flat. In a short space of time the track has descended from a primeval forest to rolling farmland; a great way to finish the ride.

Map: BB33 Hunua
Distance: 24 km
Climbing: 1200 metres
Grade: 3+
Notes: There is a camping ground at Blackberry Flat you can book into, and a picnic area with water and toilets.

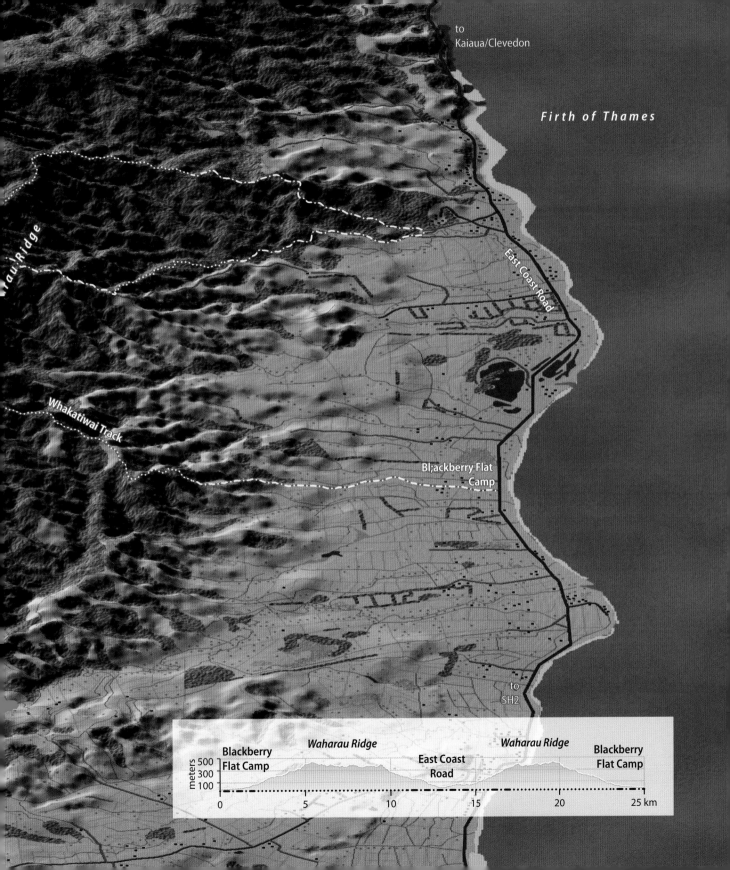

to
Kaiaua/Clevedon

Firth of Thames

East Coast Road

au Ridge

Whakatiwai Track

Bl;ackberry Flat
Camp

to
SH2

meters 500
300
100

Blackberry
Flat Camp

Waharau Ridge

East Coast
Road

Waharau Ridge

Blackberry
Flat Camp

0   5   10   15   20   25 km

THE WIRES
COROMANDEL FOREST PARK

The start of this gnarly old track is located in the Maratoto Valley in Coromandel Forest Park, before it crosses the Coromandel Range into the Wentworth Valley. It was built in the 1870s during the Waikato land wars to divert the main Auckland to Wellington telegraph line out of harm's way. Later on it became a pack track for settlers, gum diggers, lumberjacks and gold miners, and is now one of the few mountain-bike tracks into the Coromandel ranges. In the 1880s there was extensive kauri logging in the area, and most of the streams were dammed to provide enough water to transport the logs from the bush. Even the Wires Plateau was farmed in the 1920s, though it proved unsuccessful. The subsequent erosion and deforestation is now showing signs of recovery.

From Paeroa, head north for 9 kilometres on State Highway 26 and turn right onto Maratoto Road. Head east up the valley for 5.5 kilometres and turn left onto Wires Road, which you follow for a short distance to park at the Hamuti Stream ford. A swingbridge provides access when the water flow is high, but you wouldn't want to be biking up there in such conditions. The track begins as an unmaintained gravel road that passes a few farmhouses before becoming rough.

The climb up the ridge below Hikurangi (693 m) is steep and convoluted, initially on a smooth, hard-packed clay surface. This is a popular 4WD, quad and motorbike ride, with the local 4WD club providing work parties for general maintenance and drainage. They have done a great job keeping the erosion at bay in this high rainfall area. From the track there are glimpses of the bush-clad Coromandel Range and across the patchwork of farms on either side of the Waihou River.

The track becomes rocky and rougher above the 300-metre contour, with some large boulder climbs and deep ruts to test your trials skills. After reaching the ridge summit, the track descends a little to the Wires Plateau, where the original pack track joins up after ascending an adjacent northwest ridge. The track continues past Route 19 and the end of the Maratoto Loop to an old corrugated-iron shelter. There are a number of ride options from here.

If the weather has been dry, you can continue around the Maratoto Loop for a real challenge. It has some difficult rock climbs, deep ruts and holes big enough to swallow a Unimog. You won't find a gnarlier 4WD track anywhere: a sign on the gate says, 'You will sustain damage to your vehicle on this section of track.' With a mountain bike it's comforting to know that you can always carry where you can't ride. This loop really is a lot of fun and starts from just beyond the shelter.

Just past the Maratoto Loop Track, descending due east, is the walking-only section of Wires Track that goes to Wentworth. Next to it, heading south, is a very rutted and rugged trail-bike track that climbs to the top of Ngapuketurua then descends steeply to follow the Waipaheke Stream back out to Maratoto Road. Take this option only if you are prepared to carry your bike most of the way and enjoy pain and suffering, and the building of moral fibre.

It is better just to head out the way you came, enjoying the superb downhill scenery and birdlife among the regenerating forest of tawa, rewarewa, kowhai and nikau, with kanuka and manuka filling the gaps. Look out too for the old telegraph poles, mine relics and hut sites in the surrounding bush.

'You will sustain damage to your vehicle on this section of track'

Mud and rocks on the way down from the Wires Plateau

Map: BC35 Paeroa
Distance: 25 km
Climbing: 700 metres
Grade: 2–3
Notes: Impossible mud plug after heavy rain.

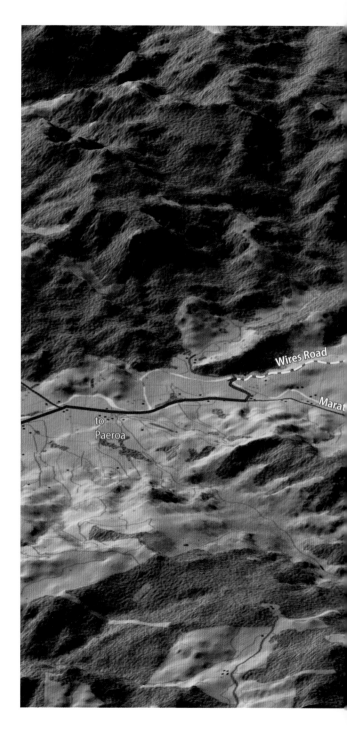

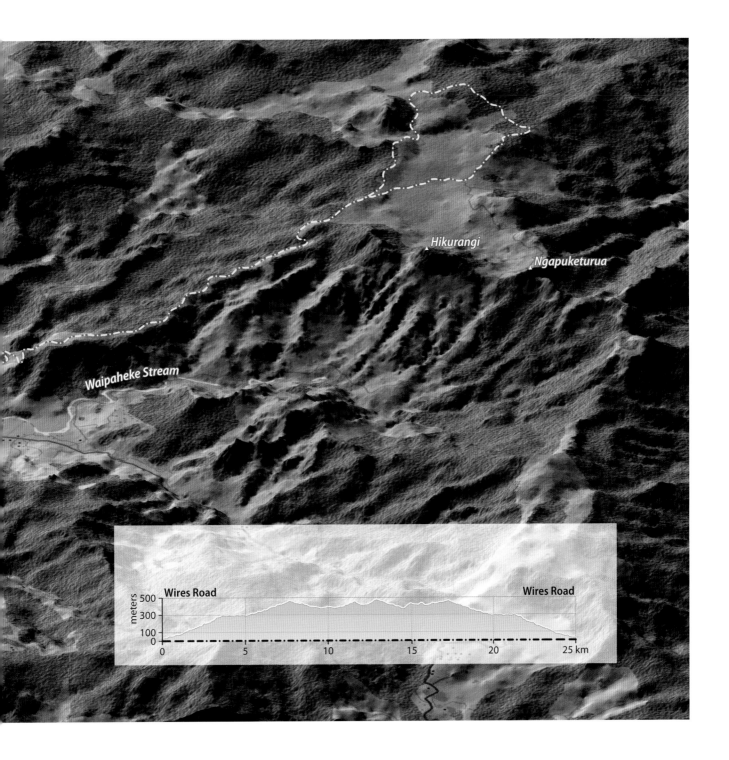

Hikurangi

Ngapuketurua

Waipaheke Stream

Wires Road   Wires Road

meters 500
        300
        100
          0
            0   5   10   15   20   25 km

OTIPI ROAD
BAY OF PLENTY

This ride lies in the backblocks of the Bay of Plenty, southeast of Opotiki, where a large road sign proclaims 'Eastland, the first place to see the sun'. Follow the Motu Road, 10 kilometres east of Opotiki, to the tiny settlement of Toatoa, then ride east on the Takaputahi Road. This remote stretch of gravel surrounded by bush heads up the Ngaupokotangata Stream and into the Takaputahi River catchment. Pockets of open country fit like a jigsaw into the thick, lush bush. Just before the bridge over the Ngaupokotangata Stream, a 4WD track, euphemistically called Otipi Road, fords the Whitikau Stream to its true right bank. This was an old hydro development road formed in 1952 when a dam was proposed on the Motu River. From the stream the track ascends steeply on a rain-rutted rocky surface with single track status just around the corner. It's a big climb to the 900-metre contour just below Otipi Peak at 958 metres. This is followed by a series of undulations with magnificent views as you ride high above the twists and turns of the remote, wild water of the Motu. It's a whitewater magnet for kayakers and rafters, who shoot the many rapids on their way back out to civilisation.

A washed out stream gully along the far end of the ridge

A Y intersection is eventually reached, with the track to the left descending towards the Motu River after crossing a large slip, beyond which single track prevails. The right track continues along the ridge top without joining the river, but offers a great view down to the river from the track end. The left track loses almost 400 metres as it sidles through a couple of rough stream gullies before popping out into partially open country near the end. The bottom section has become overgrown with gorse but it's a worthy bush bash to the Motu River beyond.

It is sobering to stand on the river flats, literally miles from nowhere, and reflect that a mere 50 years ago a mistake was almost made by damming this beautiful river. The bush is returning to the flats, as it will to the track above. If you lunch by the water you may be lucky enough to be visited by blue duck, who cruise back and forth across the rapids before settling on a large grey rock on the far bank. They are so well camouflaged as to be almost invisible.

Retrace your knobbly tracks up the gnarly climb and along the undulations in reverse for the final awesome descent back to the Whitikau Stream. Watch out for some slippery clay surfaces near the bottom—it's potential crash material.

This single track descent takes you down to the Motu River

The river flats are overgrown and wet under tyre

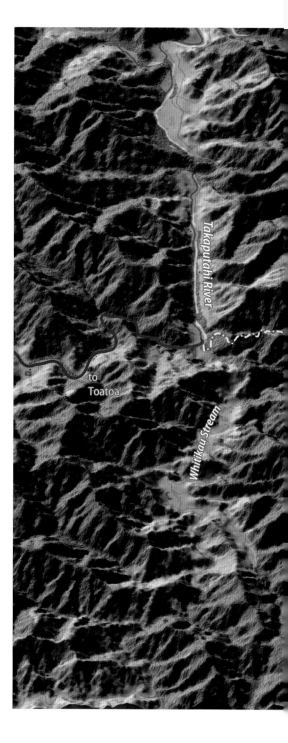

Map: BE42 Houpoto
Distance: 38 km return
Climbing: 750 metres
Grade: 3
Notes: Opotiki makes a great base to take trips from. It has lots of accommodation and all the facilities a mountain biker requires.

Motu River

Otipi

Motu River

Takaputahi Road   Otipi   Motu River

1000
800
600
400
200

meters

0   2   4   6   8   10   12   14   16   19 km

PAKIHI TRACK
BAY OF PLENTY

The remote farms of the Toatoa and Whitikau valleys were developed long before the turn of the 19th century, when sheep and cattle were driven to market in Opotiki from the top of the rugged and remote Motu Road via the Pakihi Track. This crude stock track was eventually cut and benched, and proved to be the perfect grade for mountain biking when it was rediscovered in the late 1980s. It is reputed that more dynamite per kilometre was used on the lower section of this track than on any other built in New Zealand. The profile of the track is set to be raised after being selected as part of the New Zealand Cycle Trail Project, with signage, re-benching, bridges, water control and clearing almost complete.

Head southeast out of Opotiki on Otara Road and after 14 kilometres, at the confluence of Te Waiti and Pakihi streams, turn left over the bridge and onto Pakihi Road. Follow it to the end, and the start of the Pakihi Track.

The track hugs the true left bank of Pakihi Stream as it initially travels through regenerating bush and into the virgin forest. Massive boulders dot the streambed, with steep-sided hills enclosing the valley. The climb is very gradual as the track follows the twisting stream in and out of every pleat of the landform. Many side streams tumble down from the hillsides above to race under your rotating wheels and into the main flow below. The bush is thick and lush with tree ferns, rimu, rata, tawa, beech and pockets of nikau palms and broadleaves to admire.

Eventually, after some classic leaf-littered single track riding, you cross over Pakihi Stream onto its true right bank. The stream is often so low you can boulder hop your way across, but check with DOC in Opotiki first; they may have built a bridge. A short, steep exit climbs high above the river, levelling out just above the old six-bunk Forest Service Pakihi Hut. A short switchback track drops you down to the hut clearing with its dog kennels, and there's a short track to the river's edge.

Above the hut the track climbs smoothly, tracing the hillsides through some pretty steep country. The many south-facing gullies are cool and damp, and filled with ferns and lichen. Some decent slips along the way have opened up commanding views across the primeval jungle that covers the hills and mountains below Urutawa Peak. Twelve kilometres and 430 metres of climbing later you pop out onto the Motu Road, a remote stretch of gravel in the back of beyond.

This is a good spot to refuel in the sun and prepare to enjoy the long return downhill. This flows back to the hut in style across Pakihi Stream and along the Pakihi Stream valley to the start—an awesome 22-kilometre single track buzz to end the day.

Reaching the classic Pakihi Hut, built by the old Forest Service

The track hugs the true left of the Pakihi Stream on the way to the hut

Alternatively, you can bike the newly formed Dunes Track that trundles east out of Opotiki to the start of the Motu Road, just before Omarumutu. Follow the Motu Road into the misty mountains and drop down to Toatoa. This remote gravel road then climbs up to Whitikau and drops again before finally climbing to the start of the Pakihi Track. At the bottom of the Pakihi Track exit out to Opotiki to complete the near 100-kilometre loop. There are plenty of bike shuttle and accommodation options available in Opotiki.

The beautifully benched Motu Road–Pakihi Hut section of the track

Map: BF41 Oponae
Distance: 44 km return
Climbing: 750 metres
Grade: 3

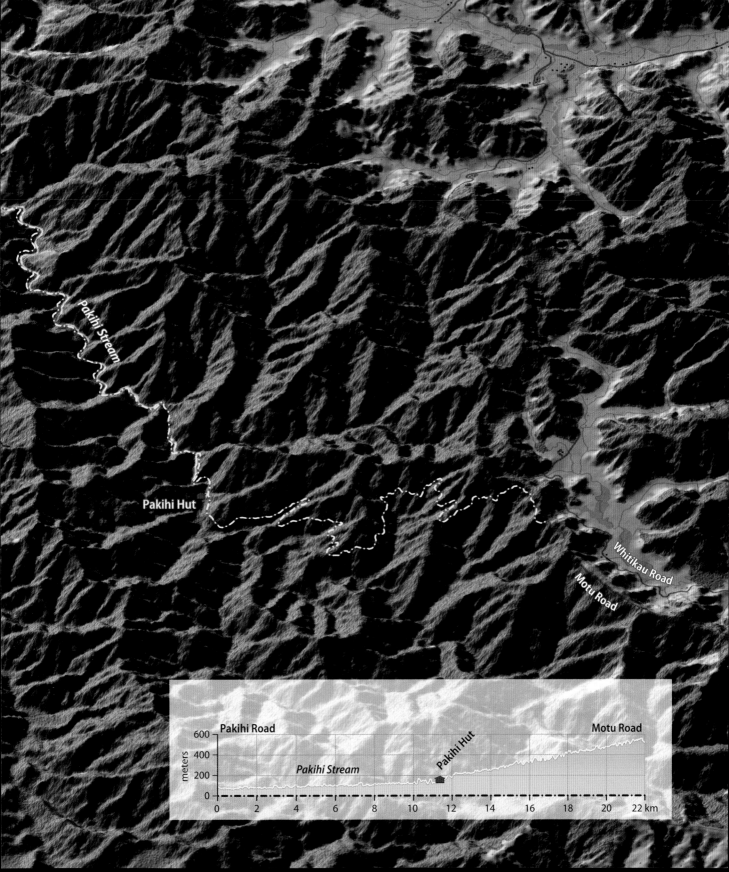

Pakihi Stream

Pakihi Hut

Whitikau Road

Motu Road

Pakihi Road   Motu Road

600
meters 400
200
0

Pakihi Stream

Pakihi Hut

0   2   4   6   8   10   12   14   16   18   20   22 km

TE WAITI TRACK
BAY OF PLENTY

Drive southeast from Opotiki on Otara Road for 14 kilometres and park near Te Waiti Stream bridge, or just before the Opaeroa Stream ford, which is straight ahead instead of crossing the bridge. Cross this ford and pedal down the narrow, winding gravel road that follows the true left bank of Te Waiti Stream. The road climbs above the river and tracks through lush semi-coastal forest, providing great views down to the stream below. After a few kilometres the Te Waiti benched track begins, signposted just before the road drops down to Bush Camp on the river flats. The track initially crosses a mix of clearings and bush blocks, before coasting into dense bush and the Urutawa Conservation Area.

This is an old pack track that has been cut and benched into some steep slopes at a gradient perfect for mountain biking. It probably serviced some early farming blocks cleared beyond Te Waiti Hut. Beech trees dominate the high canopy with tree ferns filling in the gaps. This superb piece of single track climbs steadily, crossing a number of side streams, many of them running from spectacular waterfalls. Steep drop-offs plummet to Te Waiti Stream below, with very little between the rider and the sudden effects of gravity. In the narrow sections you want to be sure of your line. All major stream crossings have been bridged, apart from the final one, with the remaining ford potentially rideable.

About halfway along you enter a part of the forest full of nikau palms, growing up in every available spot and giving a tropical feel to the bush. The track for the most part runs due south on the eastern aspect of the ranges, so it gets morning sun but little else. This keeps the bush moist and lush, but with a well-drained track the riding is rarely slow or muddy.

Eventually the track drops steeply down over a series of rocky outcrops to ford Te Waiti Stream. This can be a tricky crossing if the stream is high, but it is usually rideable. It is only a short ride from there to the spacious six-bunk Te Waiti Hut. This is used mainly by hunters and trampers and sits in the sun on the true right riverbank, making it a great place for lunch. A tramping track continues up into the catchments of both the Tokenui and Wahaatua streams if you want to explore further on foot. In fact the track that heads east goes all the way to Pakihi Hut.

The return ride is surprisingly mainly downhill, with the track taking on a different character, and the riding getting a little bit easier. This is an enjoyable and relatively easy ride for those of all biking abilities, in a stunning slice of East Coast forest.

Bridged stream crossings predominate on the Te Waiti Track

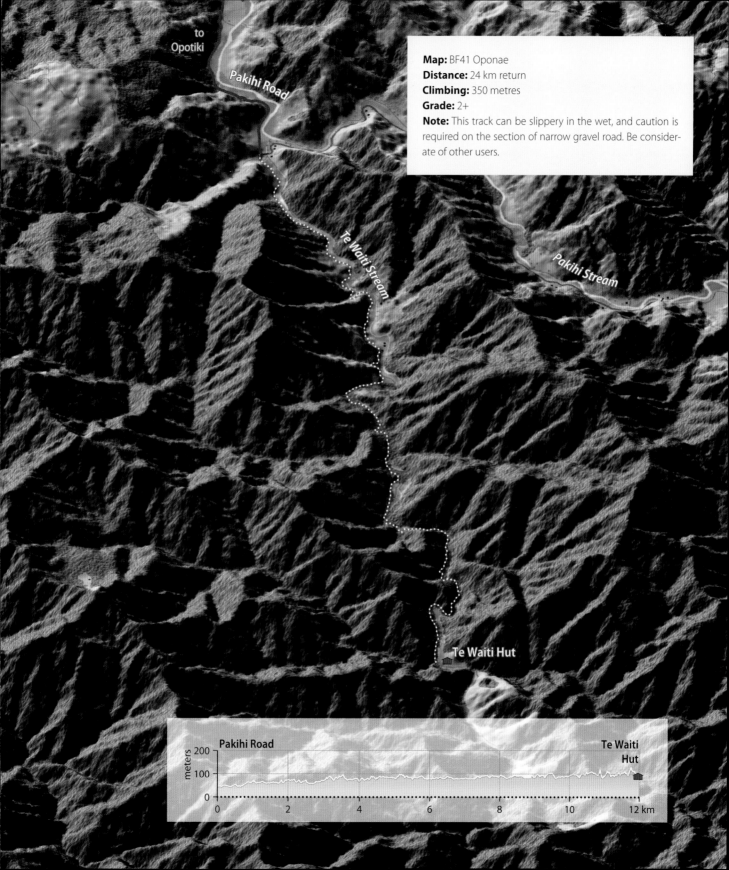

to
Opotiki

Pakihi Road

Te Waiti Stream

Pakihi Stream

Map: BF41 Oponae
Distance: 24 km return
Climbing: 350 metres
Grade: 2+
Note: This track can be slippery in the wet, and caution is required on the section of narrow gravel road. Be considerate of other users.

Te Waiti Hut

Pakihi Road

Te Waiti Hut

meters

200

100

0

0   2   4   6   8   10   12 km

Nikau palm trees provide a tropical feel to the Te Waiti Track

MOERANGI AND FORT ROAD TRACKS
WHIRINAKI FOREST PARK

The Moerangi Track was originally a tramping track that looped around a group of three huts deep in the Huiarau Ranges in Whirinaki Forest Park. It was constructed by the New Zealand Forest Service, which had its headquarters on the outskirts of Minginui to control native forest logging and exotic planting. The logging came to an end in 1987, with DOC taking over responsibility for the tramping tracks, huts and pest eradication in the greater Whirinaki Forest Park.

To get to Minginui drive along State Highway 38 to Te Whaiti and head west on Minginui Road. There are many ways to ride this track but the most popular, with the least amount of climbing, starts from the Okahu Road end carpark and ends at the River Road carpark—the best way to get there is to use the local Minginui bike shuttle service. For an overnight or return trip skirt Minginui Village, cross the Whirinaki River and make a hard left onto River Road, confusingly signposted as the Whirinaki Track, and head south along the river's true left bank to the road end carpark. This is the start/finish of the track.

For the one-way option from the Okahu Road end the track heads up the Okahu Stream, initially climbing gradually before steepening through cut-over bush to a low saddle below Koheke and Mapouriki peaks. The subsequent descent goes on forever in thickening bush, following the Whangatawhia Stream as it grows and meanders down the gentle valley. It's pure single track all the way, and vaguely follows the old tramping route but on a better grade, crossing a series of log bridges on the way down to Skips Hut. The hut is perched on a terrace next to a side stream in a large clearing—a perfect spot for the hut, which DOC has spruced up and added a verandah to.

The track continues down the valley from the hut before climbing away from the river and wandering west into the Moerangi Stream catchment to arrive at the historic Rogers Hut. This was constructed in 1952 by Forest Service deer cullers, and is built of adzed and split totara. It was subsequently named after the first child of Rex Forrester, one of the builders. The track now heads due west to climb

way above the river on a spectacular bench cut into steep ridges. Huge beech trees dominate the forest with crystal clear water running below. The Moerangi Stream loses its volume and pace before entering a small gorge at a major track confluence. A short side track leads to the newly renovated Moerangi Hut situated in a clearing, while the main track heads north along a short gorge and valley.

The gorge section has some of the most beautiful trees you will see anywhere, as the track climbs and descends through its green canopy. At the end of the short valley and gorge, the biggest ascent of the day looms, climbing steeply up a series of zigzags through cool southerly facing ridges and gullies to a high saddle just below Moerangi Peak at 1051 metres. The views are breathtaking and you get a glimpse of the dense forest that once covered the whole of the central North Island as the track traverses just below the ridge.

It's a long descent into the Whirinaki River catchment, where the track picks up a short remnant of an old logging road before diverting west into the darkest part of the ride through massive ferns and a high, dense canopy. The final climb takes you to the River Road carpark after completing the best back-country track in the North Island. Try the return trip for a whole new set of climbs, descents and stunning vistas; this can also work with an overnight stay in one of the huts along the way back.

Fort Road Tracks
DOC has also developed the Fort Road mountain bike tracks. These can be found at the far end of Old Fort Road,

The Dutch colours of the historic Rogers Hut

which starts from the same place as River Road. Drive or ride to the end, ignoring any side turns—the road is a bit overgrown and looks remote but it's only a short distance to the end. There is a 16-kilometre blue, 12-kilometre red and 3.6-kilometre yellow loop, with the blue track utilising the best bits of new single track to join up old logging roads. The single track is superb and the logging roads provide the speed. Much of the area has been logged but is regenerating well, with some very tall trees still growing in this section of forest. They are almost too big to hug. The birdlife is abundant, with kaka screeching above, flocks of parakeets racing around the lower canopy, fat wood pigeons, and North Island robins following in search of any insects mountain bike tyres uncover. This ride is a great introduction to the Moerangi Track.

Opposite *Fort Road single track amongst the rata vines and massive old growth podocarps*

Fallen giant on the climb to Moerangi Peak

Maps: BG38 Wairapukao, BG39 Ruatahuna
Distance: 36 km one way, 72 km return, Fort Road Tracks, 16 km
Climbing: Okahu to River Road 800 metres, or 2200 metres return, Fort Road Tracks 460 metres
Grade: 3, Fort Road Tracks 2
Notes: The Jail House in Minginui has rental accommodation and can organise a bike shuttle.

to
SH38

to
SH38

Minginui

Whirinaki River

Okahu Road

WHIRINAKI FOREST PARK

Moerangi

Skips Hut

oerangi Hut

Moerangi Stream

Rogers Hut

Okahu
Road

Minginui

meters							

1000

800

600

400

Skips Hut

Rogers Hut

Moerangi Hut

0   5   10   15   20   25   30   36 km

LEG BREAKER LOOP
GISBORNE

This is an excellent back-country ride on the edge of Gisborne, but it requires a permit from Hikurangi Forest Farms Ltd, and can only be ridden during weekends and public holidays. You can pick up a permit and map from their Gisborne office at the corner of Darby and Gladstone roads or phone them on 06 867 9799 and they can fax you a copy to sign. The forest may be closed from time to time if there is a fire risk.

From Gisborne, head north out of town on Riverside Road. This follows the Waimata River through the settlement of Karakaroa and turns into a smooth gravel road with picturesque views along the valley. Ride past a large native restoration project and through the settlement of Motukeo until you come to an intersection after about 12 kilometres. Continue straight ahead and after a few hundred metres go through a farm gate, around the corner of the farm and over a large metal forestry gate on your right. Select a low gear and ride uphill into a plantation of eucalyptus trees. This is the entry point into the Hikurangi Forest Farms Riverside plantation.

The forestry track initially follows the Waimata River before heading east along the Makahakaha Stream. Ford the stream 800 metres further on and pedal up Yaw Road. The road climbs through a mix of old growth forest and new planting on a little-used track where natives are reclaiming the edges. Climb to the ridge top and follow its summit on an undulating journey heading east. Tall conifers provide the pine-needle leaf litter that makes the riding very smooth and quiet, with tree ferns and their ground-hugging cousins growing between the bare trunks of the trees on either side of the track.

Ignore all side roads, staying on the upper ridge until you meet a four-way intersection. Go straight ahead onto Leg Breaker Road, which may not be signposted. The track undulates for a while along the top and arrives at a Y intersection, where Leg Breaker Road is signposted. It then blasts down a fast and slick southeast ridgeline, before peeling off at the end and dropping down to the Makahakaha Stream valley. There are farm fences, a stockyard and an old shed on the open grassy flats at the edge of the pine plantation —some of the few things that remain of the old farm that was taken over for the plantation.

Stream crossings come thick and fast as you ride west down the valley. Some are quite manageable, but most are extremely slippery, as if the bottom is covered in ice. Tall native trees have made the most of the free space around the stream way and there is a surprising amount of birdlife. Ignore any side tracks and stay in the stream until you reach the bottom of your original climb at Yaw Road. At that point go straight ahead and ride back the way you came to Gisborne.

Undulating along the summit

Mega-slippery Makahakaha Stream crossings

The old farm track roams along the valley floor

Map: BG43 Gisborne
Distance: 40 km
Climbing: 650 metres
Grade: 3
Notes: Only ride in the permitted area and be aware of other trail users.

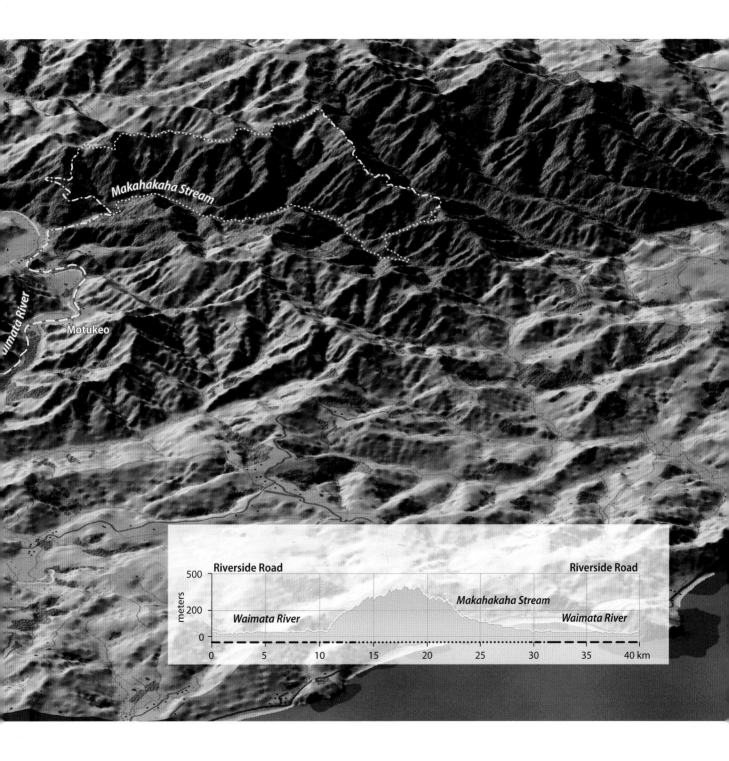

Makahakaha Stream

Waimata River

Motukeo

Riverside Road

Riverside Road

meters

500

200

0

Waimata River

Makahakaha Stream

Waimata River

0   5   10   15   20   25   30   35   40 km

OLD MAHANGA ROAD
GISBORNE

The original coastal route took travellers from Mahanga, on the east coast south of Gisborne, over the steep hills of the Wharerata Range and down into Poverty Bay. It climbs along a stretch of scenic coastline before heading inland, where the grades are more gentle and less prone to slips. State Highway 2 now turns north at Nuhaka and goes through Morere, replacing the Old Mahanga Road which has reverted into a remote 4WD farm track.

The best way to ride the old road is to get dropped off at the picnic area and lookout at the very top of the Wharerata Range. From there, pedal north towards Gisborne for half a kilometre and turn right into Paritu Road, which is signposted. This is a wide gravel road used mainly by the forestry company and the few residents along its length. The road undulates between open farmland, pockets of regenerating native bush and an extensive pine plantation in varying stages of growth and harvest.

Ignore all side roads as you cross over the Tikiwhata train tunnel about halfway along Paritu Road. The tunnel is over 200 metres below you, burrowing for 3 kilometres from the Tikiwhata Stream to the Waiau Stream. Built in 1943, it's the fifth longest in the country. This windy section of the Palmerston North–Gisborne railway has many tunnels and bridges, and was the site of the 1938 Kopuawhara disaster. A sudden cloudburst sent a wall of water surging through the public works camp at Kopuawhara and 21 people were drowned, making it New Zealand's deadliest 20th-century flood.

Enter a forestry block just past the Railway Road junction, and at the Circuit Roads turn-off, go straight ahead onto an overgrown 4WD track, passing an old homestead and a group of farm buildings. Shortly after, the Old Mahanga Road climbs up an unmarked overgrown cutting that veers left away from the main track. Follow this overgrown track into the depths of the pine forest—if you go straight ahead you reach a dead end and group of high-rise beehives.

Eventually you climb out of the forest to the edge of a farm where the track is blocked by an old gate, which is now a solid fence. Climb over this and head to the track on your left that runs down the back of some pine trees. It looks a bit vague, but you soon pick up the line of the old road as it cruises through open paddocks, descending gradually east. It traverses through some large bush blocks before revealing stunning coastal views, with the white sand of Mahanga, Pukenui and Oraka beaches stretching around to Mahia. Auroa Point and Kahutara Point can be clearly seen at the far eastern end of the bay, with their steep sea cliffs and rocky outcrops jutting into the blue ocean.

Before long you reach the first farm building, and then the main homestead and the accommodation at Mahanga. The road becomes gravel down to sea level and this marks the end of the ride. Alternatively, this ride can be done as a hill climb with the descent on the return leg, for a taste of some gnarly granny-ring climbing. Otherwise you can continue out past Lake Rotopounamu and Mahanga Beach and head right on the remote gravel Tunanui road. This travels through the Taumataoriaki foothills, farms and forestry to the hot pools and café at Morere.

Stunning coastal views are revealed as the track enters open farm country

A Mahanga-Pukenui beach backdrop

Map: BH43 Wharerata
Distance: 27 km one way, 60 km for the complete loop
Climbing: 300 metres one way, 1350 metres for complete loop
Grade: 2
Notes: For the most part this is legal road, but contact Malcolm and June Rough (Ph: 06 837 5751 or www.quarters.co.nz) at Te Au Station for access to their property. They have excellent accommodation available among shady trees close to the beach, with superb views, so this is a good place to base your ride.

Wharerata   to
                             Gisborne

Paritu Road

Tikiwhata Stream

WHARERATA FOREST

Waiau Stream

Taumataoriaki

re

Kopuawhara Stream

Lake Rotopounamu

Mahanga Beach

Pukenui Beach

Kopuawhara

Wharerata   Wharerata

600
Paritu Road   *Kopuawhara*
                                   Stream
meters 400   Morere
200

0

0   5   10   15   20   25   30   35   40   45   50   55 58 km

WAIONE TRAM TRACK
PUREORA FOREST PARK

Pureora Forest Park comprises two separate islands of forest lying between Lake Taupo, Te Kuiti and Taumarunui, totalling 78,000 hectares. The Hauhungaroa Range traverses the larger southern block, with the Rangitoto Range prominent in the northern block. The park protects some of the last podocarp forest remnants in the North Island. Podocarps once thrived in the volcanic pumice and ash soils of the central North Island, but much of the forest has been extensively logged, leaving behind a network of roads, old tramlines and skidder tracks that are ideal for mountain-biking exploration.

DOC has published a brochure with information on a number of excellent mountain-bike rides in both the north and south sections of the park. One of the best and longest rides is in the southwest corner of the forest. The track starts at Piropiro Flats, which is accessed from State Highway 30. Twenty-five kilometres south of Te Kuiti, turn right onto Waimiha Road just after Mangapehi, then right onto Poro-o-Tarao Road and finally east onto Kokomiko Road. This road travels through farming country for a while, then heads into exotic forestry blocks where it starts to narrow and feel quite remote. Persevere until you eventually reach the large open clearing at Piropiro Flats. In 1930 this was a thriving mill town with a school and a busy sawmill, which lasted until the timber ran out. Many years later the NZFS transformed it into a campsite, which DOC now maintains.

From the campsite, ride south on Totara Stream Road, ignoring all the side roads on your left, then after 500 metres turn right onto Maraaha Road. Again, ignore all side roads on your left. From the DOC mountain-bike sign at the end of this gravel road, select your lowest gear and climb directly ahead up the devilishly steep clay track known as The Panhandle. The track narrows to single track and heads into bush, following an old log recovery route towards the Maramataha Valley. Toetoe, kanuka and buddleia line the track as it descends into the native forest. Technical single track follows the Maramataha River downstream, then drops steeply down a series of switchbacks to the river below.

The ford is just above the knees in normal flow, but can be difficult or impassable after heavy rain—a wire rope strung across the river may be of assistance. Across the ford a long unrideable climb takes you up to a high terrace and into one of the most beautiful podocarp forests in the North Island. The track now follows an old haul line out into more open country, which is rapidly regenerating into bush, then onto an old tramline. The track splits here, with the left branch going to a hunters' campsite and makeshift shelter, and the right turn continuing to the main loop road junction.

A newly bulldozed track confuses the DOC pamphlet directions at this junction. In theory this is where the loop track starts, and DOC suggests you ride it clockwise. In practice it's well marked in the anti-clockwise direction, though either way is just as enjoyable. So go down the road to the right, ignoring all side tracks until you eventually pick up bright orange arrows at the bottom of the hill around Te Rerengaohore Stream. You then climb through mature bush on a well-used quad-bike track.

This track vaguely follows the black dotted line on the topo map, which up to now has been almost completely useless. It heads into open country then blasts down a fast descent lined with waving toetoe. After a couple of kilometres it intersects a wide 4WD track at right angles. Go left for 400 metres and then follow the markers onto an old 4WD track that narrows and heads south. This climbs gradually through tussock and a large group of tall cabbage trees before disappearing into the forest. Still vaguely following

Travelling open grassland above Te Rerengaohore Stream

the dotted lines on the map, the track rises and falls like a rollercoaster through a tunnel of bush. It descends and crosses the Waione River and a long line of bluffs before returning to open country.

Continue riding in a northwest direction over grassland dotted with tree stumps, dodging the blackberries along the way, down to a tributary of Te Rerengaohore Stream. A final downhill through the bush takes you back onto the new DOC 4WD track, where you go left back to the main

loop intersection. This is completely unmarked but you should recognise it. Ride back the way you came and cash in on all that climbing you did to get to the big loop. There is an awesome descent back into the Maramataha River, and the push up the other side is surprisingly short, followed by another downhill almost all the way back to camp.

This must be one of the best rides in New Zealand, despite the navigational difficulties, with plenty of riding challenges and track diversity through fantastic scenery.

Gnarly descent into the Maramataha River

Map: BG34 Piropiro
Distance: 38 km
Climbing: 1050 metres
Grade: 3
Notes: Pick up or download a Mountain Biking Pureora brochure from DOC. It describes all the good riding and other options to explore. You can return by riding the loop in the opposite direction, exploring some of the many side tracks.

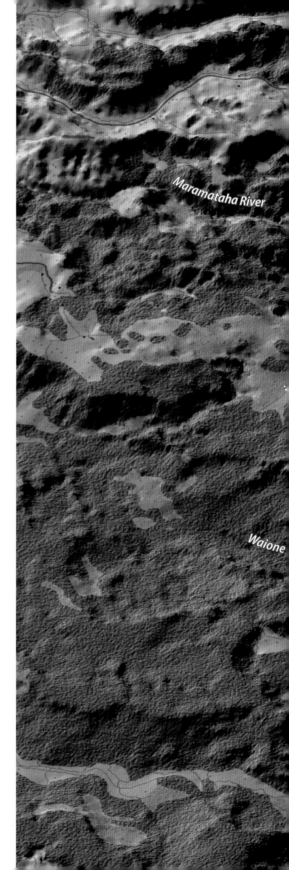

Maramataha River

Waione

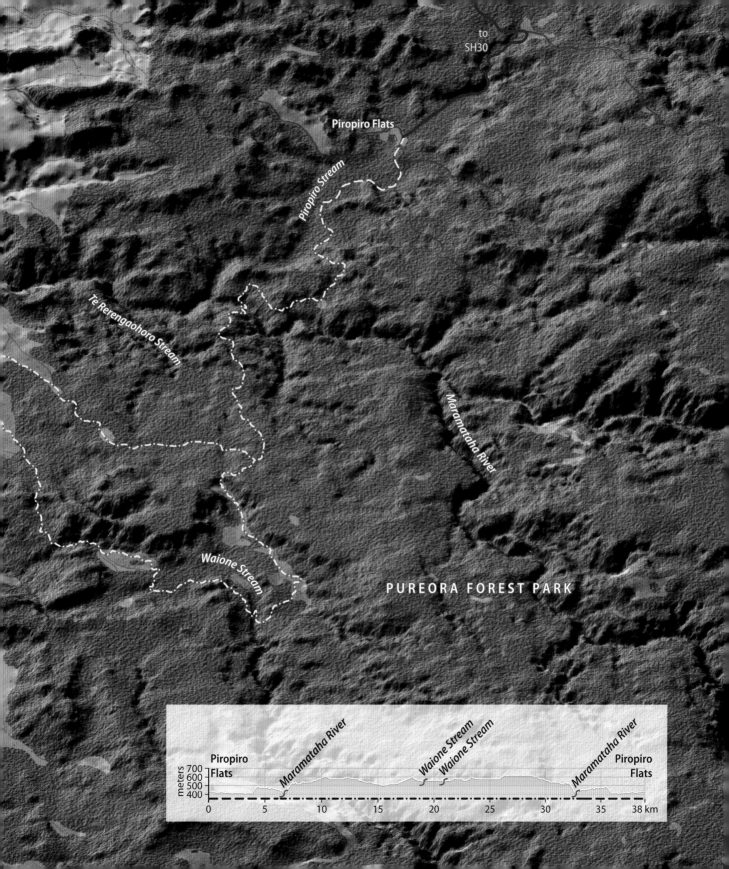

to
SH30

Piropiro Flats

Piropiro Stream

Te Rerengaohoro Stream

Maramataha River

Waione Stream

PUREORA FOREST PARK

Piropiro
Flats
Maramataha River
Waione Stream
Waione Stream
Maramataha River
Piropiro
Flats

meters
700
600
500
400

0   5   10   15   20   25   30   35   38 km

TREE TRUNK GORGE
KAIMANAWA FOREST PARK

Kaimanawa Forest Park is situated on the east side of Tongariro National Park, encompassing a large area of native forest and tussock grasslands. It is a popular fishing, hunting and recreational playground offering mountain biking, short walks and tramping trips, with picnic and camping areas available. Access is from State Highway 1, turning left 16 kilometres south of Turangi into Kaimanawa Road, then following the DOC signs and gravel road to the Urchin campsite. This is situated on a terrace high above the Tongariro River and makes an ideal spot to start the ride from.

Ride back down the gravel road for about 100 metres and go left onto the leaf-litter single track heading to the Pillars of Hercules. This amazing section of track winds down through tall beech forest around tight turns and switchbacks to the Tongariro River, where a wire swingbridge crosses high above the water, with the Pillars of Hercules below. These basalt columns are hard to distinguish from such a great height, but are spectacular when seen from close up. Beyond the rideable bridge is another short section of single track that soon joins an old 4WD track. By now the beech forest has disappeared, to be replaced by fast growing kanuka and manuka, with a variety of natives making the most of the shelter they provide.

The track heads to State Highway 1 between the Mangatawai and Mangamate streams, across a flat expanse of river terrace. At State Highway 1 ride south and climb for 2 kilometres to the left turn onto Tree Trunk Gorge Road. A smooth, fast downhill takes you to the gorge and its violent rapids. This metre-wide chute and series of waterfalls, through which the Tongariro River pummels, has claimed the lives of four rafters who missed the get-out point further upstream. The rapids were finally paddled by New Zealand kayakers in 2007, with sore bodies and bruises to show for their crazy endeavour.

Continue a few hundred metres uphill to a major intersection and head north on the Tree Trunk Gorge Track. More leaf-litter single track follows the Tongariro River downstream, climbing steeply on loose rubble to a river terrace at 700 metres. There are great views of the river, with the craters of Mt Tongariro beyond. A long, flowing downhill is followed by two stream crossings and an impressive rocky bluff that towers above the track edge. Above the bluff, a technical section next to a singing and dancing creek is all that's left of the trail, before a final climb back to camp. The bush is stunning and there's nothing better than starting and finishing a ride on an excellent piece of single track.

Ducking under a tree trunk on the Tree Trunk Gorge track

An impressive rocky bluff forces the track to take evasive action

The last few fords on the way back to camp

Map: BH35 Turangi
Distance: 20 km
Climbing: 500 metres
Grade: 2–3
Notes: Watch out for the wasps in summer and the traffic on State Highway 1.

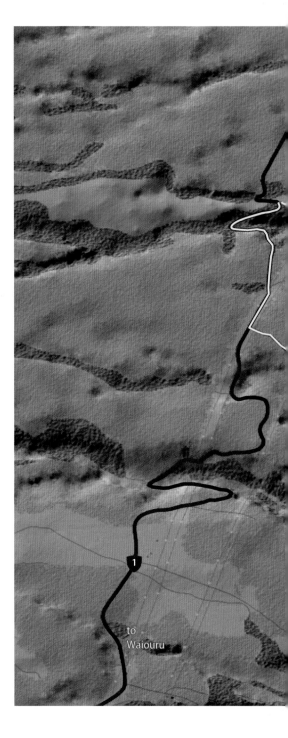

to
Waiouru

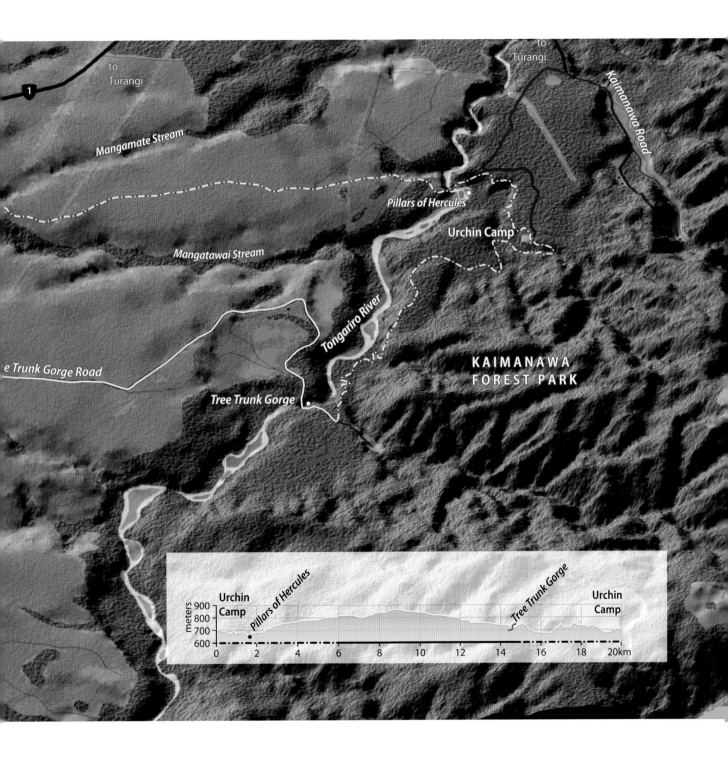

to Turangi

Kaimanawa Road

Mangamate Stream

Mangatawai Stream

Pillars of Hercules

Urchin Camp

to Turangi

Tongariro River

e Trunk Gorge Road

Tree Trunk Gorge

KAIMANAWA
FOREST PARK

meters

Urchin Camp

Pillars of Hercules

Tree Trunk Gorge

Urchin Camp

900
800
700
600

0   2   4   6   8   10   12   14   16   18   20km

TE IRINGA TRACK
KAIMANAWA FOREST PARK

Kaimanawa State Forest Park covers an area of around 77,000 hectares and is situated in the central North Island southeast of Lake Taupo. Hidden in the wet and dense bush of the park is an old pack track called Te Iringa, which runs down the east side of the Kaimanawa Recreational Hunting Block. This area was set aside in the early days of the Forest Service to control introduced animals, and to encourage this a network of tracks and huts was constructed. DOC now administers and maintains these tracks and facilities, and to their credit have re-marked old tracks and improved access in tricky situations. The park is one of the few places where sika deer can be hunted in New Zealand.

The Oamaru River valley was first associated with Maori settlement and a series of wars in the mid 17th century. The first Europeans arrived in the mid to late 1800s, with surveyors Smith and Cussen traversing the country in the 1870s and 1880s. Gold exploration also played a part in the late 1800s but was short lived. Farming was established in the surrounding valleys and fire was used to clear the land, but blocks of pine plantations surround most of the park today.

To get to the area, drive towards Napier from Taupo on State Highway 5 and turn right after about 26 kilometres onto the Taharua forestry road. A further 10 kilometres through the neatly planted rows of pine trees takes you to a right turn onto Clements Mill Road and into a tunnel of bush. Follow this narrow, winding old logging road for 5 kilometres to the start of the track, signposted just after the Te Arero Stream bridge.

The luxuriant bush is an intense green colour as you ride the first section of single track to the start of a steep climb. This heads up the ridge, over a torrent of exposed tree roots with a mix of switchbacks and rideable traverses. The top segment has some tall steps and a short washed-out carry section. The red beech that dominates the lowlands soon makes way for stands of silver beech and mountain cabbage trees.

Climb to a clearing of soft grass mowed by the local deer, where the old Te Iringa Hut used to sit. The hut was destroyed by fire in the 1980s and never replaced. The track eventually leaves the ridge and drops around its southeast side on a more gradual bench, through a series of tricky rock gardens mixed with steep drops and slippery gullies, as it skirts below the peak of Te Iringa. You eventually return to the ridge top where the terrain is more manageable.

By now all the red beech trees have disappeared and the track traverses through stands of open silver beech forest, revealing glimpses down into the Mangatoatoa Stream valley. It is virtually all downhill from here, with the track rolling through some beautiful old growth forest on a bed of crispy leaf litter. The path is well-worn, more from goats and deer than human footsteps or tyre treads. A steep slope on either side drops away symmetrically to the east and the west, defining this distinctive ridgeline. This must be one of the best downhills in the country.

A series of challenging switchbacks is encountered at the bottom of the ridge, just before the track heads southeast after crossing the Tiki Tiki Stream. Then a short but technical section of trail takes you out to the swingbridge that crosses to the true right bank of the Kaipo River. From there, spreading trees shade the smooth and fast single track all the way down the widening Oamaru Valley. The track follows the river terraces, with frequent detours back to the water's edge before heading out of the forest for good.

Pedal through a series of grassy flats that are being rapidly taken over by blocks of kanuka. Behind them, bush rises

to
Taupo

Te Iringa Hut Site & Clearing

Te Iringa

Mangataotao Stream

KAIMANAWA FOREST PARK

Tiki Tiki Stream

Kaipo River

Oamaru River

Oamaru Hut

Te Iringa
Hut Site
& Clearing

meters

Kaipo River

Oamaru
Hut

1200
1000
800
600

0   2   4   6   8   10   12   14   16   18 km

Flowing single track heads to the hut clearing

uninterrupted from the valley floor to the tops. After some great riding you arrive in time for lunch at the 12-bunk Oamaru Hut. Perched on a high terrace at the confluence of the Oamaru and Kaipo rivers, the hut commands a great view down the valley and proves a perfect spot to relax, stay the night and do some fishing, or you can ride back out and enjoy the track in reverse. This is jungle riding at its very best.

Map: BH36 Motutere
Distance: 35 km return
Climbing: 1250 metres
Grade: 3–4
Notes: With permission from Porenui Station you can head out over their land to Taharua Road and then ride north to complete the circle.

42 TRAVERSE
TONGARIRO FOREST CONSERVATION AREA

The 20,000 hectares of Tongariro Forest are wedged between Tongariro National Park and the Whanganui River to the north. National Park, Turangi and Taumarunui make up the surrounding triad of towns. Gazetted in 1900 as State Forest 42, it was systematically logged of its totara, matai, rimu, miro and kahikatea over the following decades. The Dominion Timber Company and the Egmont Box Company built large mills to process the trees, with myriad tracks and bush tramways gradually penetrating the entire forest to supply their insatiable appetite. With millions of board feet of timber extracted by the 1930s, the millable timber was all gone, and the slow process of regeneration took over.

Plans to replant introduced trees did not progress much further than a few test plots and peripheral plantings, so many of the old tracks still remain. Toetoe, cabbage trees and manuka are colonising these once wide trails, turning them into single track, though many are little more than a bush bash and will soon disappear forever. There is still a vast array of excellent tracks and trails for mountain biking. Many are loops or side trips off the famous 42 Traverse, giving access to some of the more remote corners of the forest hidden in the gullies and ridges of this convoluted landscape.

The 42 Traverse is one of the great North Island rides. Its 50-kilometre length covers a mix of gravel road, 4WD and quad bike tracks, and is best travelled from east to west due to the predominantly downward direction. The start is 18 kilometres north of National Park on State Highway 47. Turn left onto Kapoors Road, where there is a large DOC interpretation panel. This gravel road takes you past a barn to a second DOC sign with information and times for the ride. There are plenty of DOC markers en route to point you in the right direction but the track is so well worn these days it's hard to go astray. It's not all downhill, with plenty of short climbs and the odd long one thrown in, but rest assured—your exit point is almost 500 metres below your starting point.

Turn onto Slab Road, which heads north and parallel to Pukchinau Stream. The twisted remnants of old growth rimu, saved from the chainsaw by their uneconomical

shape, tower high above juveniles below. The track descends onto Magazine Road, and after about 2 kilometres a side track leads off to the right to Cooee Lookout. This provides great views into Echo Canyon and across to the volcanoes of Tongariro National Park. In the canyon the bush is lush, dense and obviously well-watered. Patches of gorse are disappearing under the progress of native regrowth, but enough remains to pierce knobbly tyres and penetrate bare skin.

Back on the main track, an incredibly long, undulating descent ensues to the ford at Bluey's Creek and Waione Stream. This is about the halfway point. The stream can get high in wet weather and parts of the track become very muddy—a sure recipe for wrecking your running gear. The climb from the ford takes you close to the snaking origins of the creek-size Whanganui River. Further along there are good views down to the river from the most northerly section of the track.

The climb around Ngapari Peak descends towards the first of many stream crossings on the way out to Owhango, including Big Mako, Little Mako and Pepenui streams. In between you pass the site of Bennetts Hut. Hook onto Dominion Road and ride to a bridge that has been blown up once, but there is a replacement to cross. Further down you can admire the 20-metre waterfall from Waterfall Bridge, set among beautiful bush. This long stretch climbs almost as much as it descends, and eventually crosses Deep Creek before a massive concrete bridge that takes you over the Whakapapa River. A final climb on a wide gravel road circles the Ohinetonga Lagoon before arriving at the Owhango township.

The hotel/cafe on the main street has coffee, ice creams, pies and all those unhealthy things you desire after a long ride. This is a good place to wait for your shuttle or refuel for the wee road ride back to the start, or maybe the reverse of the 42!

The Volcanic Plateau backdrop to the track

Map: BH32 Raurimu, or the Tongariro Forest Adventure Map
Distance: 52 km
Climbing: 900 metres
Grade: 3
Notes: National Park Backpackers (www.npbp.co.nz) have excellent accommodation and provide a shuttle service for many of the local tracks.

Whanganui River

Ngapari

**PUKEPOTO
FOREST**

Mako Stream

Waione Stream

TONGARIRO FOREST

to
Turangi

Kapoors Road

47

Owhango

Stream

Whakapapa
River

30   40   50   52 km

to National Park

TUKINO MOUNTAIN ROAD
TONGARIRO NATIONAL PARK

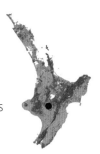

In 1887 Horonuku Te Heuheu Tukino IV, paramount chief of Ngati Tuwharetoa, gifted the three volcanic peaks of Tongariro and the surrounding land to the Crown for all New Zealanders to enjoy, thus creating New Zealand's first national park. The park now covers over 80,000 hectares and has a dual World Heritage classification recognising both its natural and cultural values.

The Tukino Mountain Road lies within the park, crossing the northern side of the Rangipo Desert. The first road, built to provide access for skiing on the eastern side of Mt Ruapehu, was constructed in the 1940s by the New Zealand Army. This was extended into the national park in the 1960s and the first ski club hut was then built on the mountain. The army set up the first rope tow in 1962 and the ski club subsequently installed one in 1966. In 1975 the Tukino Mountain Clubs Association was formed, bringing all user groups under one umbrella. Tows were re-aligned, added to and motorised, and a large lodge was built to accommodate the growing number of skiers. The access road to the skifield had a number of re-alignments over the years before the present route became established, and it now also provides a great mountain-bike ride.

The three highest peaks in the North Island are all volcanoes, with the highest being Mt Ruapehu at 2797 metres, followed by Mt Taranaki at 2518 metres and Mt Ngauruhoe at 2287 metres. In fact these are the only North Island peaks over 2000 metres, so it's not surprising that all three attract a fair bit of bad weather; the compensation is the outstanding views they provide on a clear day. They are all active volcanoes, with Mt Ruapehu erupting in 1995 and 1996 and spewing ash over the surrounding countryside. The frequent volcanic activity in the area inhibits the regrowth of vegetation and is responsible for the surrounding desert.

The Tukino Mountain Road heads west from State Highway 1 (Desert Road) 31 kilometres south of Turangi. It is well signposted with a large Tukino Skifield sign. The initial flat stretches are on fine river stone and soft sand as the track makes its way between the first colonisers of the fertile new ash laid down by the eruptions in the 1990s. Toetoe are the tallest of these, with scrubby, ground-hugging alpine plants in the majority. Ruapehu's snowfields feed numerous

The initial climb up from the Volcanic Plateau

Ruapehu's summit from the road end

side streams where plant life is far more prolific. The Upper Waikato Stream is crossed very early on in the ride and the stream carries on to join the Tongariro River.

North of the road and sheltered from the worst of the weather, dracophyllum and stunted totara cover the endless corrugated ridges. The track leaves the windswept flats and begins to climb the lower slopes, where a moonscape of eroded gullies covers the mountain, sculpted by wind and rain. There are excellent views of the remains of the summit plateau glaciers, which are retreating as the decades pass. Now in the shadow of the mountain, you are protected from the worst of the prevailing westerlies and southerlies, and you can often see long trails of fast-moving cloud skirting the mountain and heading away while you ride in full sunshine.

The ski road steepens into a gnarly 4WD track as it climbs up a long ridge into the barren desert country surrounding the peak. The views are superb, especially looking back the way you came across the gullies and streams circling the lower slopes. On a clear day Mt Ngauruhoe's cone pierces the clouds to the north, and further along the volcanic chain Mt Tongariro is often visible. Massive ramparts of twisted rock, which have been flung from the crater, fan out to the northeast with streams running at their feet.

The final stretch takes you through the alpine village and down to the base of the steep boulder face below the lower ski tow. At over 1600 metres this is probably the highest point you can climb off-road on a mountain bike in the North Island. The spectacular country above can be accessed easily on foot, and you can even venture up to Ruapehu's summit. A large waterfall roars down from above and you can follow its progress over a series of drops while walking alongside the tow. There are plenty of good spots for lunch before bombing back down the ski road or cruising down to enjoy the view.

Twisted rock below Mt Ngauruhoe

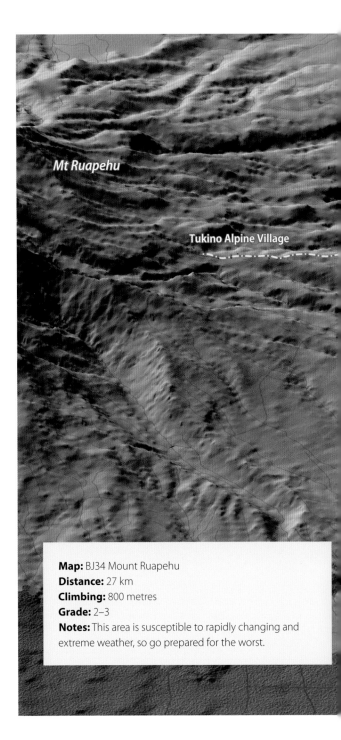

Mt Ruapehu

Tukino Alpine Village

Map: BJ34 Mount Ruapehu
Distance: 27 km
Climbing: 800 metres
Grade: 2–3
Notes: This area is susceptible to rapidly changing and extreme weather, so go prepared for the worst.

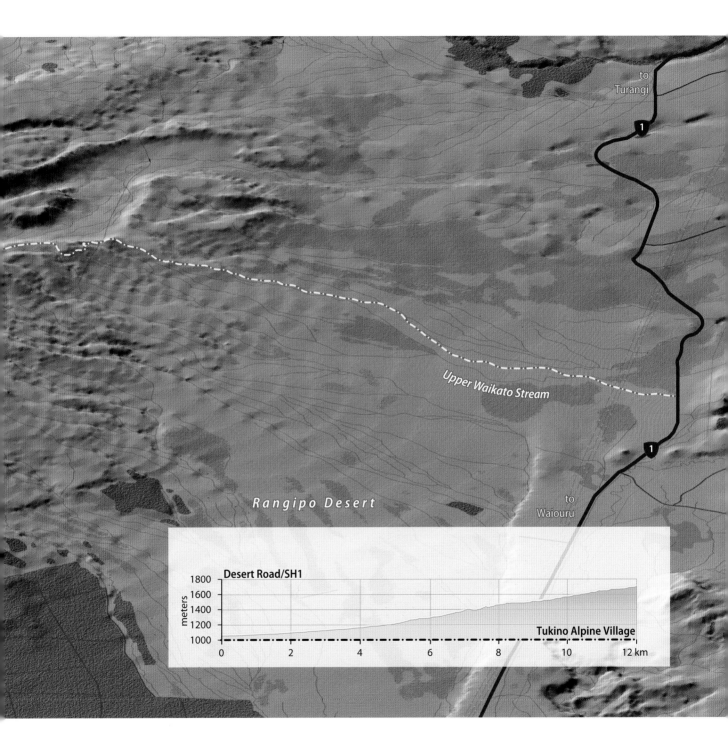

to
Turangi

1

Upper Waikato Stream

1

to
Waiouru

Rangipo Desert

Desert Road/SH1

1800						
1600						
1400						
1200						
1000						Tukino Alpine Village

meters

0   2   4   6   8   10   12 km

WAIKATO RIVER TRAIL
TAUPO

New Zealand's largest lake, Lake Taupo, is the source of New Zealand's longest river, the Waikato. As it travels its winding route to the sea, the Waikato River is slowed by a series of man-made lakes and dams, feeding nine power stations that are the cornerstone of the North Island electricity network. The Waikato River Trails Trust had the vision for a multi-use trail following the river for 100 kilometres from Lake Atiamuri to Lake Karapiro, near Cambridge. With funding from the local community, trusts and companies, much of the proposed trail has now been built or connected to existing tracks.

Access is via State Highway 1, travelling north from Taupo to Atiamuri Dam and then left on State Highway 30 to Whakamaru Dam; or south from Matamata on State Highway 1, turning right at Tokoroa on State Highway 32, which also heads to Whakamaru Dam and the start of the ride. There is a fantastic lakeside reserve and camping spot just east of the dam. The trail heads through this reserve near the lake edge and below tall pines, with spectacular rocky outcrops directly across the lake below Whakaahu Peak and further around toward Te Rakau Creek. At the very end of the reserve the Ongaroto Bluffs section starts.

This section is pure single track benched into the bush at the lake edge, a rollercoaster ride sandwiched between the road and the water. Short, steep climbs are matched with long, flowing downhills and bermed corners among beautiful bush and gnarly old pine trees. Views of the lake are never far away, and before long you are riding below the vertical Ongaroto Bluffs. After a very steep climb, a razor ridge is descended via a tricky staircase where, for your own safety, you should push or carry your bike to the trail below.

The track eventually drops into the Whakamaru Christian Camp, which is situated across a short causeway on Hikurangi Island in the river. It then heads through farmland and onto the Dunham Creek Mobility Trail. Boardwalks and smooth gravel wind through the wetlands next to the river, ending at a small road reserve. The trail then ducks back into the bush, re-emerging to travel a short section along the road edge. Before long you are back riding incredible single track on copper-coloured pine needles above a hard clay and sandy base.

This last section of track reveals views up the wide, slow-moving channel of the river to the towering rocky outcrop of Pohaturoa, its lower slopes cloaked in pine forest. The trail is now a blast through a plantation or on the river edge, where gnarly old-man pine trees are growing among the regenerating native bush, sending their roots across the track like octopus tentacles. Follow the yellow-topped track markers along the edge of a couple of open paddocks, under the Tram Road bridge and back onto single track.

The final few kilometres of trail follow the river past Pohaturoa to State Highway 30, before joining State Highway 1 just before the Atiamuri Dam. Check out the dam over lunch, and for those keen to ride back down the trail, your reward will be an afternoon of single track riding on what feels like a different trail.

Superb lake-edge single track around the shores of Whakamaru

Exotic leaf-littered trail heading to Pohaturoa

Map: BF36 Whakamaru
Distance: 43 km return
Climbing: 500 metres
Grade: 2
Notes: Check out www.waikatorivertrails.com for the latest on new trails, maps and donations to the cause.

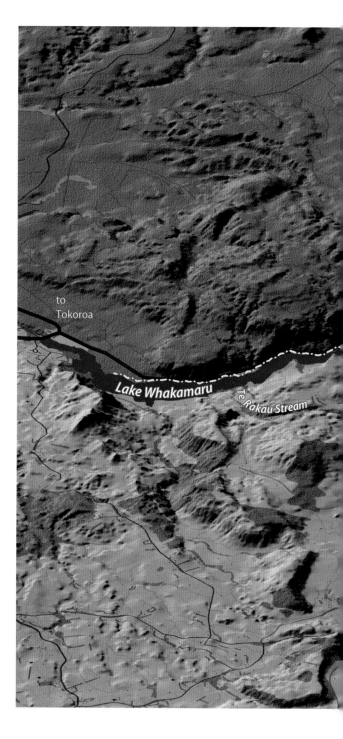

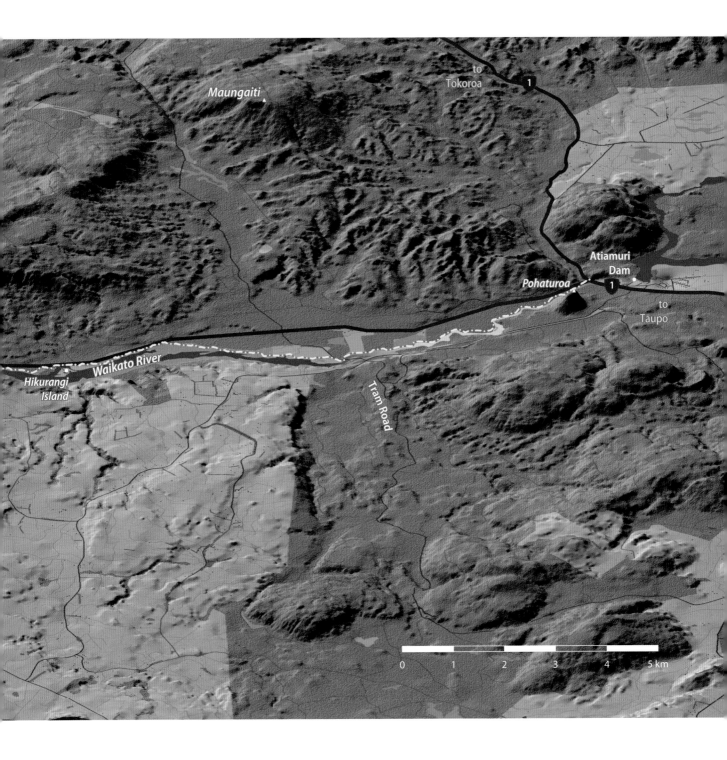

Maungaiti

to
Tokoroa

1

Atiamuri
Dam

Pohaturoa

1

to
Taupo

Waikato River

Hikurangi
Island

Tram Road

0   1   2   3   4   5 km

W2K AND K2K TRACKS
TAUPO

The W2K Track is a middle-chain-ring ride for the fit, running from Whakaipo Bay, on the edge of Lake Taupo, west to Whangamata Bay and the village of Kinloch. A dedicated band of cyclists from the Bike Taupo Club built this amazing track, and their names are fittingly carved into a wooden table at the highest and furthest point of the track. The track is a work of art, with its flowing cambered corners, short downhills and swooping turns; its gradual ascents and descents are interspersed with switchbacks, and there are plenty of obstacles and speed control built into the natural terrain. There is no relaxing if you want to extract the most from this ride, but it can also be cruised at a more gentle pace, making it suitable for riders of all levels.

From Taupo, head southwest along Acacia Bay Road to its end, and onto Mapara Road for another 6 kilometres to the DOC Whakaipo Reserve turn-off on your left. At the grassy flats by the lake edge continue to the west end of the bay to the start of the W2K Track. Cross the stile, hop on your bike and pedal through open farm country into regenerating native bush. The climb takes you gradually up the ridge that overlooks the bay and juts out into Lake Taupo. The track has been benched into the slope, allowing for good water control, and is built in such a way as to control riding speed and reduce erosive braking. This contributes to a superb ride with lots of flow and change of direction.

Climb to the ridge top at 700 metres and go left to ride the Headland Track. This was completed in February 2009 and is attractive in two ways. Firstly, it's a great 10-kilometre stretch of track that weaves through manuka, kanuka, pittosporum and broadleaves with snatches of views out to the lake. Secondly, the track deceptively seems to be doing very little climbing, with the second half a rollercoaster downhill ride that seems to go on forever before magically rejoining the main track, without any more climbing. A long downhill and traverse drops you into the beautiful Whangamata Bay. The local café and store at Kinloch is a tempting spot for refreshments.

The newly benched K2K track was completed in late 2010, and is a similar ride to W2K and goes to Kawakawa Bay. It initially skirts the grassy flats along the lake edge, then ducks into the bush and climbs vigorously above a broken series of bluffs around Te Kauwae Point. There are a number of stream crossings on the way, with the 500-metre ridge top being reached rather rapidly. The descent consists mainly of leaf-litter single track that flows into Kawakawa Bay. Some camping spots and a DOC toilet can be found in the shady bush at the edge of the lake. This is a good spot for a swim.

The return ride is no less captivating, with the lure of an ice cream at the Kinloch dairy or coffee and cake at the café. Back onto W2K for the second climb of the day, you can take the Short Cut Track instead of the Headland Track to shorten the return. It takes you quickly to the top of the ridge and back into Whakaipo Bay after a blast of a descent and some great late afternoon views.

Lake views from Te Kauwae Point

The breathtaking Headland Track is well worth the extra effort

K2K, so smooth and so fast

Map: BG35 Tihoi; the track is also marked on a pdf download from www.biketaupo.org.nz
Distance: 55 km return
Climbing: 1200 metres
Grade: 2
Notes: These two tracks will eventually form part of the proposed Lake Track. This will extend a further 65 kilometres to the Waihaha Bridge on State Highway 32, making it the longest stretch of mountain bike single track in New Zealand. Donations for the fantastic track-building efforts and ongoing maintenance will be gratefully accepted by club members, and can be sent to Bike Taupo Advocacy Group, PO Box 1850, Taupo 3351.

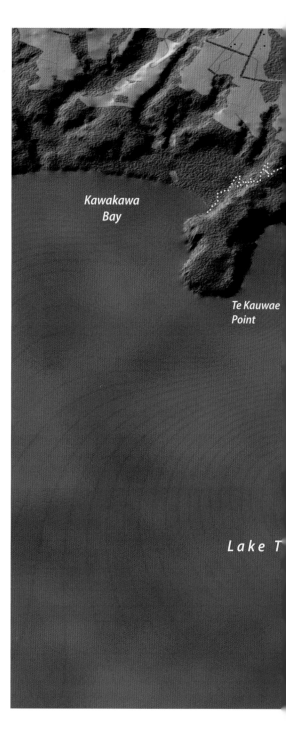

Kawakawa
Bay

Te Kauwae
Point

Lake T

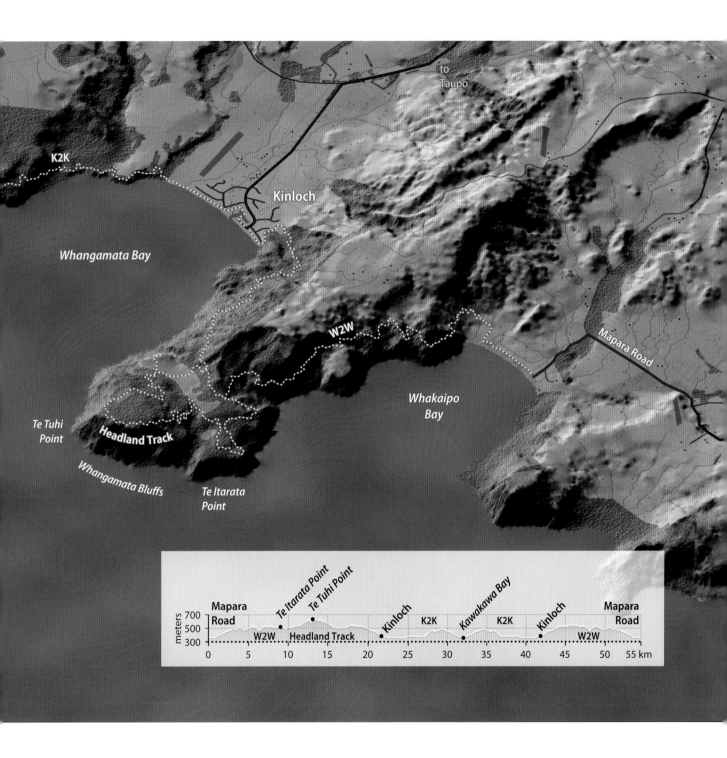

K2K

Whangamata Bay

to Taupo

Kinloch

Te Tuhi Point

Whangamata Bluffs

Headland Track

Te Itarata Point

W2W

Whakaipo Bay

Mapara Road

meters

Mapara Road

W2W

Te Itarata Point

Te Tuhi Point

Headland Track

Kinloch

K2K

Kawakawa Bay

K2K

Kinloch

Mapara Road

W2W

700
500
300

0   5   10   15   20   25   30   35   40   45   50   55 km

MYTHICAL MOKI AND REREKAPA TRACKS
TARANAKI

When mountain bikers first started riding in the Whangamomona area, the ride in was over a narrow, winding goat track that threaded its way through a Hobbit-like land to the ghost town of Whangamomona. The world had moved on and passed this bit of Taranaki by. Its shops from a bygone era were long shut, with flaking paint and faded sign-writing, and dismantled, rusting cars lay abandoned in the street. The logs had run out, the sawmill closed down and the railway just passed through without any trains stopping. The pub with its crooked verandah and corrugated iron exterior showed the only sign of life, though it too had seen better days and many more patrons, drunks, fights and dogs.

Today a sealed road leads into town and the feeling of remoteness is not so apparent, with a sign proclaiming 'Welcome to the Republic of Whanga'. The old pub sports a recent lick of paint and is now the centre of the Republic. It is still a great place to glean some local knowledge and to sit in the sun under the verandah and enjoy your favourite refreshment. There is an immaculately groomed camping domain just around the corner from the hotel, and this is the place to base your rides from.

The Mythical Moki track has a reputation for not existing. This may be due to its impassable state for many years and the fact that it doesn't join up on the topo map. The Rerekapa Track is the natural return route, turning a great ride into an even better loop. Travel 20 kilometres north from Whangamomona through broken farmland, then turn left onto Moki Road and right at the T intersection onto Mangapapa Road. This takes you to the DOC picnic area just before the Waitara River bridge. There are three old sawmill boilers and display signs adjacent to the carpark from where you start the ride. These tracks are best ridden in the dry and can be done in either direction, though there is a slight advantage to travelling clockwise, with a bit more downhill single track.

Pedal back down the road and turn right onto Moki Road. The gravel road soon turns into a clay 4WD farm track as it heads downstream on the true left bank of the Waitara River. Opposite the track thick, impenetrable bush climbs into the Moki Forest. The river has cut deep into the papa clay and its steep-sided banks provide no access to the copper brown flow below. There are a few short, steep climbs on the way to the farm hut at the edge of the Makino Forest.

From the hut an old sledge track enters the selectively logged forest, where the lack of tall timber is immediately apparent. Tree ferns dominate alongside the track, with gullies of broadleaves and clearings invaded by manuka. The riding is technical as you leave the dotted lines of the topo map and enter uncharted territory, sidling below the unseen Mt Ararat. DOC has recently marked the track, and the Forest Service previously bridged the deep side streams with short, ground-hugging swingbridges and the lesser streams with more conventional wooden bridges. Travel would not be possible without these structures.

Sections of this narrow bench are perched on near vertical clay slopes, which plummet to the log-jammed water below as the track nears the Makarakia Stream confluence. Relax and concentrate on the path ahead and not the drop below. The track soon exits the forest over the fifth and final swingbridge back onto a 4WD farm track that matches the previous side. Wind your way out of the valley and through a unique tunnel that has been cut through a low ridge in the middle of the Mironui Reserve. Shortly beyond the tunnel, the track crosses the river and joins Rerekino Road. Turn right and continue up Moki Road.

Twin falls of the Waitara River

Mironui Reserve Tunnel

This gravel road with sealed uphill sections takes you through remote farming country to a T intersection where you go straight ahead and onto Kiwi Road. Follow the Moki Stream for most of the way up the valley, losing it only on the sealed climb to the final saddle. Descend on a loose surface into the Mangatuna Stream valley. The Rerekapa Track is signposted on your right and follows Pararani Stream through farmland and back into native forest. The track can be muddy and slippery in places, with some seriously challenging ride sections up to the low saddle hiding deep in the bush.

The subsequent downhill is a lot of fun, and all too soon you reach the historic 12-bunk Boys Brigade Hut, surrounded by grassy flats, manuka and kanuka trees. The hut is now managed by DOC, and has been renovated with a new Pioneer log burner installed for those cold winter nights and renamed Rerekapa Hut. From the hut you ride through a forest of manuka on what was once an old quad bike track that was originally a logging track. Solid wooden bridges span the streams and boardwalks take you over the muddy patches until you reach farmland again.

The final section is a mix of clay and gravel, exiting back onto the Mangapapa Road just north of the DOC rest area and starting point. Turn right to complete the loop after a mythical adventure through some fantastic country.

Riding edges above the Makarakia Stream confluence

Map: BH31 Whangamomona
Distance: 46 km
Climbing: 800 metres
Grade: 3–4
Notes: Please leave gates as you find them. May be closed for lambing in the spring. Not a recommended ride in the wet.

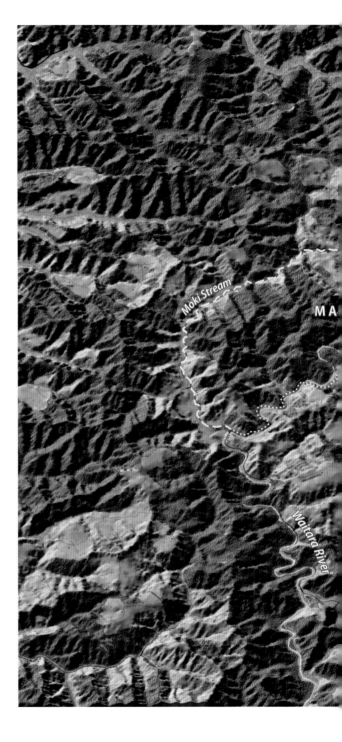

Mangatuna Stream

Blankett Creek

Rerekapa Hut

Makarakia Stream

Waitara River

FOREST

MOKI FOREST

Waitara River

Moki Road

Mt Ararat

Waingarara Stream

to Whangamomona

MAKINO FOREST

meters

400
300
200
100

Moki Road

Waitara River

Moki Stream

Rerekapa Hut

Moki Road

0   5   10   15   20   25   30   35   40   45 km

WHANGAMOMONA ROAD
TARANAKI

Whangamomona Road follows the Whangamomona River from State Highway 43 to the remote valley of Aotuhia, which was settled in the early 1900s. The only overland access at that time was a rough pack track cut through dense bush from the Whanganui River. By 1914 a road of sorts had been completed down the Whangamomona River, and it was upgraded over the following years, so for a short time Aotuhia became a thriving settlement. However the combination of its remoteness and the great depression saw many leave the community. In 1937 the 'Bridge to Somewhere' was constructed over the Whangamomona River in the hope of opening up the surrounding country for farming. The original road link proved unreliable, with slips and washouts closing it for long periods, and it has now reverted into a rugged track perfect for mountain bikes. In 1985 an alternative road was built via Makahu to allow farming redevelopment in the area.

From Whangamomona, bike south on Whangamomona Road past the old cemetery. The road soon turns from gravel into a goat track and follows every twist and turn of the Whangamomona River. There are many goats roaming this bit of Taranaki and they can often be spotted on the track or in clearings across the river. At the Poarangi Stream confluence an ancient swingbridge crosses into a farm block that heads for a few kilometres up the valley—both have seen better days. The clay track is a popular 4WD track but is almost impossible to bike in the wet. Thick, gluggy clay clings around knobbly tyres, bringing all forward motion to a halt. Even after extended dry spells you can encounter large puddles and huge bogs, but these are usually easily bypassed.

A few old telegraph poles can be spotted on the river side of the track as it heads through a mix of regenerating forest and open clearings, before you reach the first tunnel cut through clay to bypass the snaking river. There is a second tunnel soon after, followed immediately by a substantial iron bridge across the Arnold Stream, with a derelict Series 1 Land Rover, dating back to the 1950s, standing in the paddock beyond. Similar bridges cross the Miro and an unnamed stream as the track climbs above the main river on a steeper slip-prone section of the old road. This section is well forested, with regenerating native bush slowly filling in the gaps.

Thick rainforest covers the ridge tops of the Whangamomona and Okara forests as they in turn follow the river down on its true left bank. Just before the Aotuhia Quarry the track enters open farmland for the last short stretch to the Bridge to Somewhere. If you have seen the Bridge to Nowhere in the Mangapurua Valley, you will recognise its twin. Its reinforced concrete structure is almost 40 metres long, and a similar height above the river flow. Flood debris has lodged itself just above the main arch a few feet from the carriageway.

The bridge is a great place to have lunch in the sun before heading back the way you came, or for a long loop, head across the bridge and onto Okara Road, which soon bears north following Kuri Stream to a ford. The 4WD farm track from here is a legal road that follows the stream north to the edge of the Okara Forest. A tight, winding trail hugs the base of the bush-clad western ranges to finally meet up with an old dry-weather road. You then climb gradually through a long corridor of bush blocks and farm country

Corduroy punga logs form the surface of the muddy exit from the ride's first clay tunnel

Retired Series One Landrover just above the iron Arnold Stream bridge

up to a 350-metre saddle. The track wanders around the edge of Canoe Flat before dropping spectacularly down to the Tangarakau River. At the confluence with the Putikituna Stream you reach the metalled Putikituna Road and head west on a rollercoaster ride to Ohura Road and State Highway 43, just below the sale yards at Kohuratahi. Spin southwest on the tarmac back to Whangamomona. Both options provide great riding through some amazing country.

Map: BJ31 Strathmore
Distance: 40 km return, 60 km loop
Climbing: 400 metres
Grade: 2–3
Notes: This track is deadly in the wet, unless you enjoy mud.
The Aotuhia Valley end of the track is closed for lambing in the spring.

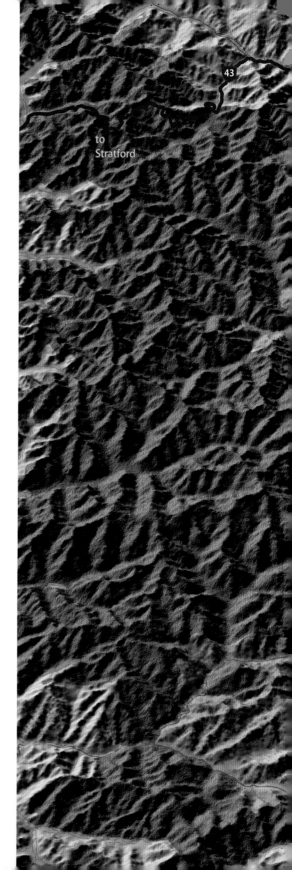

to
Stratford

43

to
Taumarunui

Whangamomona

WHANGAMOMONA
FOREST

Poarangi Stream

Canoe
Flat

Stream

OKARA FOREST

Kuri Stream

Whangamomona River

Bridge to
Somewhere

Whangamomona

Arnold Stream

Bridge to
Somewhere

meters
200
150
100

0   2   4   6   8   10   12   14   16   18   20 km

MANGAPURUA AND KAIWHAKAUKA TRACKS
WHANGANUI NATIONAL PARK

Returned servicemen from World War 1 were offered land in the Mangapurua and Kaiwhakauka valleys, and had started clearing the dense bush from their holdings by 1917. With rudimentary access to this hilly and remote piece of country, life was tough, but access was improved with a wooden swingbridge over the Mangapurua Stream, connecting the community with the riverboats bringing supplies up the Whanganui River. With intense government lobbying, a concrete replacement bridge was built, and the track was upgraded into a road.

Mangapurua Track

Unfortunately, the soils of the valley were not fertile enough to sustain long-term farming, and by 1942 most of the settlers had walked off the land. The 'Bridge to Nowhere' remains a monument to those who tried and failed. The old route is now a remote jungle ride into the heart of Whanganui National Park on a road that has evolved into single track for most of the way. The track travels through abandoned farm settlements to the graceful arched bridge, before finally reaching the Whanganui River at the Mangapurua Landing.

From Raetihi on State Highway 4 go north for 3 kilometres and turn left onto Ohura Road. At Orautoa the road veers left across the Orautoa Stream and becomes gravel. It turns left again at the settlement of Clanogan, and carries on to Ruatiti, where you go straight ahead onto Ruatiti Road. This takes you to the signposted start of the Mangapurua Road and track, which climbs gradually for a few kilometres on the old legal road, surrounded by a mix of partially cleared marginal farming country and small blocks of native bush.

You soon reach a Whanganui National Park sign, and from there the track wanders along the ridge top. After crossing the Mangapurua Saddle, bear left at the Y intersection as the bush closes around you and an intimate downhill begins. The track clambers around the true left of the upper catchment of the Mangapurua Stream on Burman's farm, sidling closer to the water flow as it descends to Slippery Creek and the Walsh farm. Large clearings of long grass are becoming surrounded by the ever-encroaching manuka, tree ferns and rewarewa. Plaques with the settlers' names mark their homestead sites, along with a few farming relics that have survived the decades of sun, wind and rain.

The track then follows the true left bank of the Mangapurua Stream, turning in a steady arc between Johnson's and Bettjeman's farms to head south before following a series of ridges to Cody's farm, opposite the aptly named Currant Bun Bluff. There are good views down to the snaking river, which has cut a gorge through the valley, with tree ferns dominating the ridges and riverbanks. Waterfall Creek is soon crossed on the way down to the indomitable Battleship Bluff, a massive papa bluff that steps vertically down to the river. The trail becomes very narrow and exposed in places as it makes its way around a series of papa bluffs with the stream at times 70 metres below.

Bennett's farm lies deserted but for an old plough on the final stretch to the Bridge to Nowhere. This art deco steel-reinforced concrete structure with fluted balustrades was fabricated at great expense in 1936, spanning 34 metres and standing 38 metres above the water. It is a work of art that carries the Historic Places Trust Category 1 rating, and had received substantial repairs in 1996. Only a short stretch of track remains between the bridge and the Man-

Bridge to Nowhere, monument and work of art

gapurua Landing on the Whanganui River, and this section heads from the bridge into tall forest before dropping down to the water's edge.

You can hitch a lift down the river or ride back out and enjoy what feels like a completely different track. There are plenty of camping spots on the way if you have a tent and are geared up for a night out.

Kaiwhakauka Track

This provides an excellent alternative route onto the Mangapurua Track since DOC embarked on a track and bridge upgrade of both tracks. To get to the start, turn right 2 kilometres south of Owhango on State Highway 4 onto the endless Oio Road. Head straight through the settlements of Kaitieke, Retaruke and Maungaroa to Wades Landing and the Whakahoro Campsite. Bike west beside a huge U-turn of the Whanganui River, then south to follow a farm track down the Kaiwhakauka Stream valley. There are fine stands of tawa and podocarp forest mixed with open flats. You soon reach the Whanganui National Park boundary where the ridges and gullies are covered in thick bush. Swing-bridges cross many of the side streams on the way to the end of the valley, from where you climb on a benched and well-graded track to the Mangapurua Track junction just past the Mangapurua Trig. Head right on the Mangapurua Track to the Bridge to Nowhere as described above.

The massive Battleship Bluff

Maps: BJ33 Raetihi, BJ32 Pipiriki, Whanganui Parkmap
Distance: 74 km return, 16 km Kaiwhakauka Track
Climbing: 950 metres return, 500 metres Kaiwhakauka Track
Grade: 3, 2–3 Kaiwhakauka Track

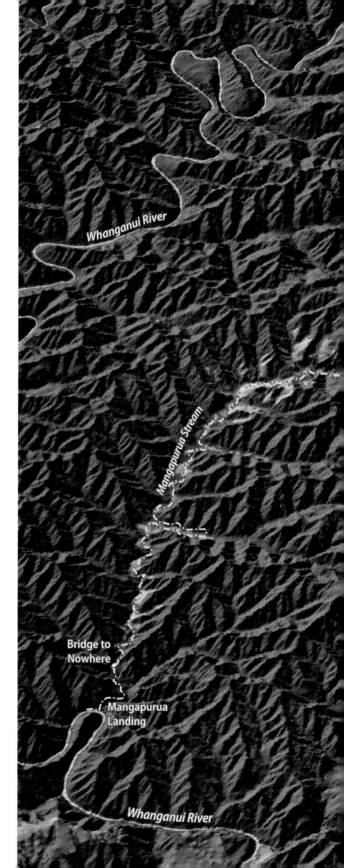

Whanganui River

Mangapurua Stream

Bridge to Nowhere

Mangapurua Landing

Whanganui River

Wades
Landing

Whakahoro

to
Owhango

Oio Road

Kaiwhakauka Stream

...purua Stream

Mangapurua

Ruatiti Road

to
Raetihi

Ruatiti
Road

Mangapurua

Whanganui River

meters

700
500
300
100

Mangapurua Stream

Bridge to
Nowhere

0   5   10   15   20   25   30   37 km

TAKAPARI ROAD
RUAHINE FOREST PARK

The 94,000 hectares of Ruahine Forest Park stretch from the Taruarau River in the north down to the Manawatu Gorge in the south. This rugged set of bush-covered ranges is subject to a fair bit of bad weather, strong winds, high rainfall and plenty of snow. So consider yourself very lucky if you strike a sunny, windless day, or even part of a day, on the tops. It is not surprising that there's a massive wind farm at the southern end of the Ruahine Range. Takapari Road was built from the NZFS Pohangina base camp to service logging on the lower slopes of the ranges, and then extended up and along the ridge top.

Head to Ashhurst on State Highway 3, then turn north onto Pohangina Road and after about 11 kilometres go right onto Pohangina Valley East Road. Takapiri Road then turns off to the right 5 kilometres past Komako. The road is narrow and follows a small stream for just over a kilometre. Park adjacent to the first gate adorned with a big DOC sign. Please leave all gates as you find them.

The legal road climbs gradually at first through picturesque open farmland on a narrow, gravel base. It soon steepens as it heads to the park boundary, giving excellent views of the Pohangina River and valley below. From the park boundary, select granny gear and head into the forest on the steep 4WD track. The lower slopes are a mixture of regenerating rata, pepper trees, flax, toetoe and a few remaining large podocarps, while the middle section is covered mostly in cabbage trees and mountain cedar, with flax and toetoe alongside the track. As you pedal past the 900-metre mark, the cedar and cabbage trees all but disappear, replaced by hardy leatherwood scrub and stunted dracophyllum hidden in the sheltered spots.

A tramping side track heads off this main route, plummeting north to Centre Creek Biv, and after a series of undulations as you gradually climb to 1100 metres, another heads south to Diggers Hut. On a clear day there is an uninterrupted view across the entire North Island, from the east coast to the west. Continue to the A Frame Hut, also called Travers Hut, resplendent in red and exposed to every possible weather atrocity Huey can muster. It's a great place if you need to shelter for lunch, or longer. A desperately steep tramping track plummets east down to the picnic area at the end of Tamaki West Road and may make a quick escape route in an emergency.

From the hut the track winds along the ridge top, sheltered in part by a double hedgerow of the tough and hardy leatherwood that grows just a metre high. The track surface quickly deteriorates into gnarly 4WD mode, climbing and descending on a surface sculpted by high water flows, wind and unmaintained drainage. This ridge-top track heads south for almost 5 kilometres, ending in a swamp after traversing the highest and most exposed section of the southern Ruahine Range.

The return ride provides a series of challenging and gnarly climbs that are impossible in high winds, culminating in an awesome downhill made the more pleasurable by the suffering and sacrifice of the climb up. Descend with care as a 4WD vehicle may be coming up around the next corner.

Descending one of the sheltered bush-clad gullies beyond Travers Hut

Wind-blown Ruahine ridge top

Map: BM35 Woodville
Distance: 37 km return
Climbing: 1500 metres
Grade: 3–4
Notes: Be prepared for sudden and extreme weather changes and take lots of spare clothing and plenty of food. Clay surfaces can be greasy in wet weather. Leave gates as you find them.

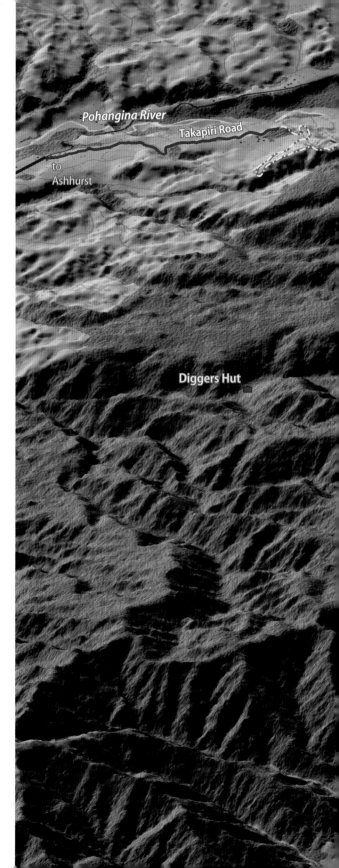

Pohangina River
Takapiri Road
to Ashhurst
Diggers Hut

Centre Creek Biv

Takapari

Travers Hut

Tamaki River

Takapiri Road

Travers Hut

meters

1300
1100
900
700
500

0   2   4   6   8   10   12   14   16   18 km

YEOMAN'S TRACK
RUAHINE FOREST PARK

Yeoman's Track lies at the eastern edge of the 94,000-hectare Ruahine Forest Park, which was gazetted in 1976 to provide conservation and recreation opportunities in Hawke's Bay. The track is an old log-hauling route that once supplied Yeoman's Mill on the flats beside the Makaroro River. The mill ran for 30 years, processing over 50 million board feet of podocarp logs from the surrounding forest. Logging ceased in 1960, and the rolling country between the river and Yeoman's Track was planted in exotic species, while the area beyond was left to regenerate back into native forest. A rusting boiler and its fallen chimney are all that remain of the mill, and the flats now serve as the road-end carpark and start of this ride.

Access is from State Highway 50, turning west onto Wakarara Road and driving to the road end beside the Makaroro River. Hop on your bike here and ford the river to the opposite bank, where an overgrown track climbs over a slip and up to the main forestry block above. Turn right onto the gravelled Wakarara Road and ride through an avenue of pine trees on a typically wide forestry road. The track heads northeast below the forested Wakarara Range before dropping down through native bush blocks and stream gullies. Ignore Moore and Leatherwood roads on the way through, but turn left down Ellis Road.

Ellis Road heads west to the historic Ellis Hut, the oldest hut still standing in the park, which was built in 1884 and restored in 1995. It is also known as Murderer's Hut

after providing refuge to accused murderer Jack Ellis in 1904. A short hill-climb from the hut takes you to the start of Yeoman's Track. This begins as two wheel tracks going up through an open cutting, then disappears into the native forest to become a shady, leaf-littered trail. The track follows the lower contours of the 1200-metre ridge above, wandering in and out of every stream gully, many of which are bridged. The regenerating bush has narrowed the trail in many places to single track, and in a series of short climbs and descents it gradually follows Dutch Creek back to the Makaroro River.

Red beech has recovered rapidly in the area, where large stands were logged in the early days for fence posts, and totara, rimu, rata and matai are slowly returning as well. Spectacular ferns cover the shady, damp spots, with toetoe quickly colonising the recent slips. After a fantastic section of riding, the track finally joins Makaroro Road for a short stint on gravel back to the river and your original ford crossing. Alternatively, you could head west up Makaroro Road instead, past an old hut site and into the upper Makaroro riverbed, if you fancy a longer ride and a bit of river riding back to the start.

Left *Historic Ellis Hut, built in 1884*
Opposite *Heading down to the first of many stream gullies along Yeoman's Track*

Dodging the windfalls just past Ellis Hut

Map: BK37 Tikokino
Distance: 24 km
Climbing: 500 metres
Grade: 2
Notes: Be considerate of other track users and watch out for any forestry activity while in the exotic forest. High rainfall can make the initial ford impassable.

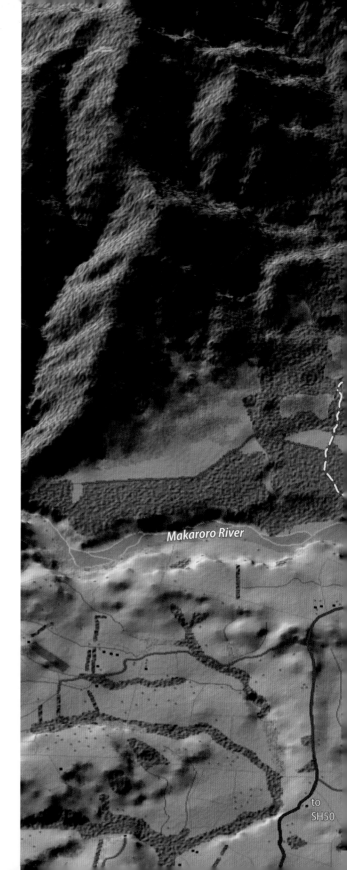

Makaroro River

to SH50

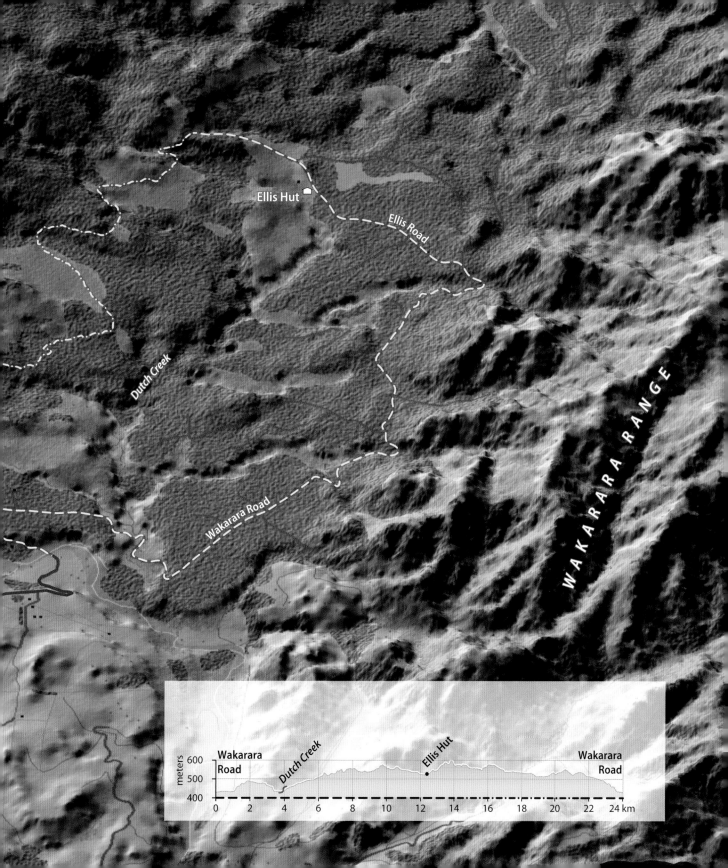

Ellis Hut

Ellis Road

Dutch Creek

Wakarara Road

WAKARARA RANGE

meters	Wakarara Road	Dutch Creek	Ellis Hut	Wakarara Road
600				
500				
400				

0   2   4   6   8   10   12   14   16   18   20   22   24 km

MT THOMPSON
HOROWHENUA

From Levin go south on State Highway 1 for 16 kilometres and then head over the railway lines east onto North Manakau Road. This road wanders up a green farming valley and after a few kilometres drops down to DOC's camping and picnic spot by the Waikawa Stream. This is the best starting point for the loop ride over Mt Thompson in Tararua Forest Park. Head south through the reserve and cross the Manakau River on a broken concrete-bottomed ford. A narrow, metalled forestry road climbs through a mix of species to an intersection where you head left up Judd's Road to climb steeply through a forestry block. Most of the trees have been harvested, with replanted seedlings already showing rapid growth. Stay on this main track as it climbs the north ridge of Mt Thompson, passing a number of side roads and skidder sites before transitioning to a dirt track flanked by regenerating bush. This track soon narrows as you ascend to the 600-metre ridge top, ignoring any tracks on your left. Thick bush has re-established itself on either side of this old track, after selective logging during the last century.

A steep and bony 4WD track now heads directly up the final part of the ridge to Mt Thompson. It is rocky and slippery in the wet, and a real challenge to ride when dry. A side track near the top branches off to the 709-metre summit of Mt Thompson, giving great views down to Levin and the Horowhenua coast. The main track continues south over a mix of surfaces from thick leaf litter, clay and rocks, and through a tunnel of bush where even dappled light is hard to come by. Bellbirds, fantails, tui and riflemen are a common sight, with native wood pigeons swooping through the lowland forest.

Occasional slips open up views across the Waitohu Stream to the adjacent virgin forest-clad ridges and tops, revealing plenty of untracked tiger country in the surrounding hills and valleys. For the most part the track is well graded, descending gradually and crossing few contour lines on the topo map so consequently having to follow the convoluted landform. It hugs the south side of the ridge so is generally cool and damp. Side streams are numerous, but easily crossed where the original watercourses have filled

Climbing the north ridge of Mt Thompson

with debris or washed out. These side streams in turn flow into the northeast catchment of the Waitohu Stream.

An impressive and fun descent ensues at the 400-metre mark, with challenging rock gardens, water ruts and wash-outs to negotiate on the helter-skelter ride down to the flats below. On the lower section you descend through tall natives and trial plantings of eucalyptus, macrocarpa and pine. Slow down for the Taranaki gate through which you enter rough farmland. The track continues down the true right bank of the Waitohu Stream, crossing the river into the farm proper. It's a short ride out to the quarry road but beware of diggers and big trucks and note the cool Tonka Toy steam shovel abandoned close to the quarry.

Turn right at Waitohu Valley road and ride back to State Highway 1, ignoring all side roads. Cross the main trunk line and turn right again on State Highway 1, travelling back to North Manakau Road to complete the loop.

Top Track views down to the Waitohu Stream valley
Above Please shut the gate mate – A FARMER

Regenerating forest surrounds the track just below Mt Thompson

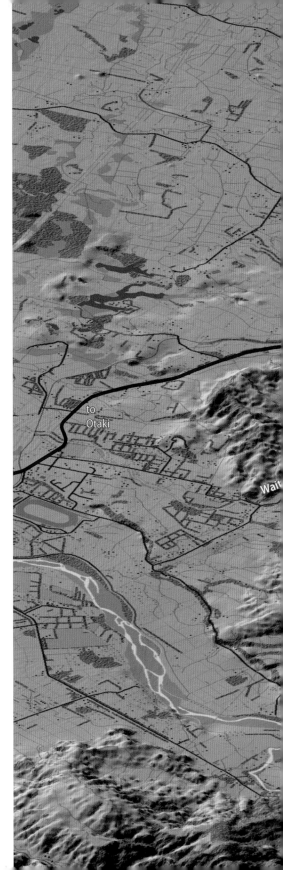

Map: BN33 Levin
Distance: 26 km
Climbing: 750 metres
Grade: 3
Notes: There are a few red-topped track markers along the route, generally just after dubious side tracks. Some are hard to spot, being partially enveloped by bush. The track goes up a grade after rain and becomes slippery and interesting to ride. Can be closed from time to time when forestry work dictates.

to
Levin

1

North Manakau Road

Manakau

South Manakau Rd

oad

Waitohu Stream

Thompson

North Manakau
Road

Thompson

Waitohu
Stream

North Manakau
Road

Manakau

800
600
400
200
0

meters

0   2   4   6   8   10   12   14   16   18   20   22   24   26 km

WAIOTAURU RIVER VALLEY TRACK
TARARUA FOREST PARK

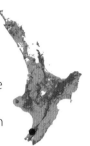

Paul Kennett pioneered this ride in the southwest corner of Tararua Forest Park in the mid 1980s, intending to use it instead of the Karapoti course, though fellow mountain bikers talked him out of it at the time, fearing it would be too hard. A limited amount of alluvial gold mining took place along the Waiotauru River, with an extensive logging operation stripping out the millable trees. This allowed farming to be established, but the upper flats have long been retired, and thick, lush bush is returning vigorously.

Take Reikorangi Road out of Waikanae, turn onto Akatarawa Road and climb up to Akatarawa Saddle. From here you can pedal northwards on Waiotauru Road, which is a disused forestry track, the cutover bush now showing signs of recovery on either side of the potholed clay surface. Ignore all side tracks as you climb steadily to the Kakanui Peak corner at 822 metres to enjoy a panoramic view across the imposing Tararua Range.

The doggedly steep slopes above and below the road are covered in gale-flattened bush, and mist often swirls around the peaks, creating a scene of primeval splendour. The track now levels out to Maymorn Junction above the flowing fingers of the Ngatiawa River. The Renata Ridge tramping track takes off along the ridge tops from here to Dress Circle, where it joins the Southern Crossing route to Field Track, ending at Otaki Forks and the junction with the Waiotauru River.

The mountain bike route continues on the only 4WD track, a rough track down to the Southern Waiotauru River where you might find alluvial gold. The Waiotauru Hut is soon reached, a squalid site where mounds of vehicular rubbish have been left and rusty steel beams litter the riverbank just below, remnants of an old logging bridge dismantled by nature.

Head further down the track to the ford, where manuka and beech shade the river as it runs clear and clean over a stony bottom, looking remarkably like a South Island river valley. A vague double track then exits the true right riverbank opposite a big slip just below Kapakapanui Peak. It's fairly important not to miss this one, as grovelling around in the riverbed to Waiotauru Forks is a cold and wet option. Climb the overgrown, slippery track out of the river, toetoe fronds invading your personal space with each pedal stroke.

Quad bikes have kept this section of track open for a short distance, but when the track starts heading up the Snowy River look for a cairn. A vague and overgrown single track slithers beside the creek in a procession of switchbacks to the Waiotauru Forks and a high wire swingbridge. The rocks, trees and swingbridge in this little gorge are very reminiscent of the South Island's West Coast. Beyond it, technical single track through tree ferns ensues over the rotting, sweet-smelling leaf litter that lies on oozy black soil. The climax is a large slip and bike carry section that really makes South Islanders feel at home, before you end up back down on the river terrace.

The valley is by now widening out, with open flats fringed by bush. The remains of an old steam sawmill lie opposite Sheridan Creek, with an impressive cast iron flywheel and steam boiler left in place to rust away. Beyond the mill a fast-flowing kilometre of single track brings you out to Otaki Forks camping ground, where a smooth gravel road exits past the ranger's house and Parawai Lodge.

Turn west onto the spectacular Otaki Gorge road as it enters the foothills of pine plantations and farming subdivisions. The Otaki River flows deep and slow below, with clear pools and swimming holes to tempt you in summer. If you haven't arranged a car shuttle, the back roads to Waikanae will return you to the start of the Akatarawa Road. A gradual, snaking ascent climbs above breathtaking views of the coast as you ride back up to the saddle to close the loop.

The Waiotauru Forks high-wire swingbridge act!

The main ford below the Waiotauru Hut

Maps: BP32 Paraparaumu
Distance: 26 km, 65 km loop
Climbing: 550 metres
Grade: 3–4
Notes: Ramps up a grade with a wet track.

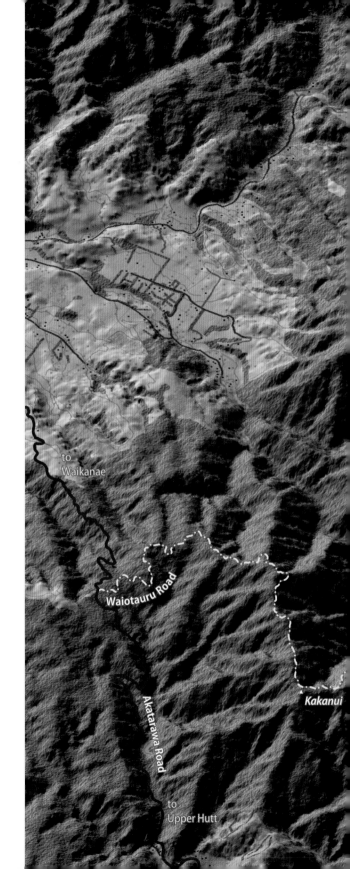

to
Otaki

Otaki Forks

Waiotauru River

Sheridan Creek

Waiotauru Forks

Eastern Waiotauru (Snowy) River

▲ *Kapakapanui*

Southern Waiotauru River

■ Waiotauru Hut

**Maymorn
Junction**

Elevation profile

meters		

Akatarawa Road · Kakanui · Maymorn Junction · Waiotauru Hut · Waiotauru Forks · Otaki Forks

900
700
500
300
100

0   5   10   15   20   26 km

GLENDHU COASTAL TRAIL
WAIRARAPA

Glendhu Station is situated at the end of a long, narrow and winding gravel road that carries little traffic, and in itself is a worthy mountain bike ride on a sunny day. The farmhouse and accommodation enjoy a sheltered spot above the Pahaoa River just a couple of kilometres from the coast. This area has been farmed for over a century but still has plenty of bush blocks, tall trees and native birds. The area feels remote and inviting, just ready to be explored over a long weekend. A self-contained bunkhouse is available or there is a place for campervans or pitching a tent.

From Martinborough, take the Masterton Road past the golf course and then turn east onto Hinakura Road. At the Hinakura settlement go south onto Bush Gully Road and then east onto the metalled Pahaoa Road and follow it almost to the sea. Finally turn right across the bridge at the Glendhu Station sign. The ride starts adjacent to the bunkhouse and follows Glendhu Creek to the banks of the Pahaoa River and out to the coast on a 4WD farm track. The coast is littered with shallow reefs and rocky outcrops—a nightmare for early mariners. The track curves around the bottom of a long ridge that marches up the coast before heading inland. Another steep 4WD track follows this ridge, while the coast track wanders past the Glendhu Rocks and a small crib protected by a rock wall and tall, shady ngaio trees.

The track then follows close to the sea and along a stretch of white and grey rock outcrops, jutting out at peculiar angles. There are a number of small streams trickling down from the hills, where small patches of bush thrive and gnarly cabbage trees make the most of the irrigation. Baches and cribs are dotted along this coast, perched among the rocks or just alongside the water. This is a popular fishing and diving coast, with crystal clear water on a pebbled beach with easy access.

A sandy section precedes a short climb onto a grassy flat, which affords stunning views up and down the coast. It's a popular spot for the station's cattle and sheep, which no doubt also enjoy the vista. The track descends to cross Waiuru Stream, and soon after passes a side track that climbs steeply towards the tops. The coast track eventually leads to the station's boundary fence, where it turns west and climbs into the foothills to ultimately join with a network of inland farm tracks. Park your bike at the boundary and cross Waihingaia Stream onto the Honeycomb Rock Walkway that leads into the neighbouring property.

A poled route heads over to the coast and along a small wetland to the Tuvalu shipwreck site. The hull and bow of the ship are visible around low tide and you can scramble over the rocks to the backbone of the ship. It sank in 1926 adjacent to Honeycomb Rock and since then has been battered and broken up by many a passing storm, with red rust eating away at the remaining steel work. A bit further around the bay are some more fascinating rocks and a large seal colony. The section of track to Honeycomb Rock is the most interesting part of the walkway and makes a good turnaround point, being only a short walk from the Glendhu Station boundary.

The return bike trip reveals all those hidden corners, rock outcrops and valleys you didn't get to see on the way in. The salt sea air is invigorating, so take time to picnic, relax and explore the rocky coast or maybe indulge in a spot of fishing. Undoubtedly this track has some of the best coastal scenery in New Zealand and is worth every pedal stroke.

Above right *Descending from a great viewpoint halfway up the coast*
Right *Coastal rocks mix with crystal clear water*

Stunning rock formations dominate the coastline

Maps: BQ35 Te Wharau, BQ34 Martinborough
Distance: 40 km
Climbing: 255 metres
Grade: 2
Notes: For accommodation and riding permission, call Kate and Jason on 06 308 8839 or Jeanne Dirderich on 06 308 8841. There are many other riding options in the foothills on both sides of the Pahaoa River.

Waihingaia Stream

Waiuru Stream

Honeycomb Rock

| 0 | 1 | 2 | 3 | 4 | 5 km |

KIRIWHAKAPAPA–MIKIMIKI TRACK
WAIRARAPA

Kiriwhakapapa Road heads east 15 kilometres north of Masterton on State Highway 2. At the road end there is a DOC campsite and reserve where the Kiriwhakapapa Track starts. From the campground the old Mikimiki tramline track heads into a tunnel of gorgeous bush following the Kiriwhakapapa Stream along the valley floor. From the early 1900s to the end of World War 2, rimu, totara and red beech were extracted from this area on a network of wooden rails and milled locally. Horse, steam and tractor power were all used in the process. The regenerating bush has almost erased the evidence of logging, with mature beech trees, rata, tree ferns and broadleaves all adding to the track's leaf-littered surface. There are strategically placed bridges across some of the trickier side creeks but little sign remains of the tram track base or rails.

Where the rail line ended, a narrow, well-benched pack track ascends from the valley floor. It's a steep climb on the bike, but the excellent surface provides sufficient traction if the legs are willing. Switchbacks add to the challenge as you climb to the 450-metre saddle. This crosses the southern ridge of Te Mara Peak on the Blue Range, which lies at the eastern edge of Tararua Forest Park, separated from the Tararua Range by the Waingawa and Ruamahanga rivers.

Wooden rail remnants on the track as it heads to the base of the climb

A tricky crossing of the Mikimiki Stream

The descent sidles as steeply as the climb, zigzagging its way down into the Mikimiki Stream catchment, where the southerly aspect creates a cooler, damper and greener ride. Tall beech forest now dominates as the track gathers pace and loses its rocky beginnings, curving east through a tunnel of bush to the water's edge. As there is no bridge you will need to ford the Mikimiki Stream, which can be tricky riding across its rough and bouldery riverbed.

The track continues down the true right bank of the stream below stands of massive beech trees. Some new bridging and track realignment finally takes you out of the bush and onto an old 4WD forestry track. This soon enters open farmland, and shortly after arrives at the track end and Mikimiki Road carpark.

There is a good spot for lunch by the river before you turn around and pedal back out the way you came in. It's like riding a whole new track when done the other way around, and that steep hill isn't as bad as it looks. If you have had enough single track for the day, you can head out on Mikimiki Road then turn north on State Highway 2 for 4 kilometres before the left turn back down Kiriwhakapapa Road to your starting point.

Switchback descent from the saddle

Map: BP34 Masterton
Distance: 20 km
Climbing: 650 metres
Grade: 3
Notes: There is a great DOC camping spot at the end of Kiriwhakapapa Road. Be considerate of other track users and avoid riding in the wet.

BLUE RANGE

Mikimiki Stream

to
SH2

Kiriwhakapapa Road

Kiriwhakapapa Stream

Mikimiki Stream

Mikimiki Road

to
Masterton/SH2

Kiriwhakapapa Road   Mikimiki Road

600

meters

400

200

0   2   4   6   8   10 km

SUTHERLANDS TRACK
WAIRARAPA

Aorangi Forest Park lies between Martinborough in the north and Cape Palliser in the south, covering a large part of the Aorangi Range. To get there, drive south from Martinborough towards Palliser Bay and Whangaimoana. As you descend to Te Kopi, the rugged coastline comes into view, with the sea crashing against the rocks and clusters of classic Kiwi baches perched precariously along the edge of the coast. It is easy to miss the DOC camp hidden from view on the banks of the Putangirua Stream, where a tent site at the bush edge on green grass can be had for only $6 a night. DOC rates this as a 'basic' campsite—there are good toilets but no running water, just the adjacent stream.

A large DOC sign halfway around the loop road behind the Te Kopi settlement announces the start of Sutherlands Track, also know as the Aorangi Crossing. The track climbs steeply, so you will have to grovel in granny gear up a ridiculously steep climb far too early in the morning for your own good. Farm tracks should be more relaxing, but this section is a taste of things to come. Crest the flat terrace and negotiate your way through a large open paddock, watched by sheep. The view around Whangaimoana Beach to Lake Ferry and beyond, offset by the deep blue sea and band of white surf, is truly spectacular.

A short climb then takes you into a pine and eucalyptus forest of dubious quality, with trackside gorse out of control. At the first intersection an old forestry map and sign obscured under the gorse shows the route going straight ahead. The track races steeply downhill to ford the remains of the Hurupi Stream, where you can attack the nasty climb on its far bank. The bulldozer driver must have had his sights on the steepest track record when he blasted through this piece of country.

You then climb a series of short, steep undulations along the ridge to its eventual top and a chance to relax in the sun, refuel and take in the ever-expanding view. On a clear day you can see the bush-clad Aorangi Range stretching out to the northeast, with the Rimutaka Range and Lake Wairarapa to the northwest, and turquoise sea and the hazy outline of the South Island to the southeast beyond Palliser Bay.

The track now follows the contours below the tops, ducking in and out of every gully, with native bush to the south and hilly sheep country with remnants of regenerating bush, bright yellow tussocks and dry grasses to the north. A final rocky climb swings around to the damp and cool southern aspect, where you begin climbing into a fascinating forest of ancient trees and ferns to the 700-metre contour and a good spot for lunch.

The descent to Sutherlands Hut is pretty dodgy; it starts off well but soon degenerates into a boulder-strewn abyss. Mountain cabbage trees adorn the edge of the track and towering beech trees dominate the view. You bottom out adjacent to Sutherlands Hut where the 4WD track fords the Turanganui River East Branch and follows it out to Waikuku to pick up the metalled Haurangi Road.

On the return ride you should be desensitised to the grade and can almost enjoy climbing the bits you had come down earlier. Back at the day's first intersection head left, through wall-to-wall gorse for a few hundred metres before regenerating beech and kanuka shut out the light. A great little track then follows the ridge to a vertiginous viewpoint above the Putangirua Pinnacles. These towers of river rock and gravel have formed because the rocks above the layers of sediment were more resistant to erosion, creating their unique shapes. Retrace your tyre tracks back to the intersection and head downhill to the start of Sutherlands track and camp.

Putangirua Pinnacles – more than just a movie set

From camp you can head up the Putangirua Stream to the base of the pinnacles, where reputedly one of Peter Jackson's early movies, Brain Dead, was filmed. You can wander among these giants, with the occasional eerie rockfall a reminder of their inevitable demise.

A gnarly climb to test the legs back up from Sutherlands Hut

Map: BR33 Ngawi
Distance: 50 km return
Climbing: 2300 metres
Grade: 3+
Notes: Take plenty of food and water, as the Aorangi Crossing is an advanced ride that involves many challenging hill climbs.

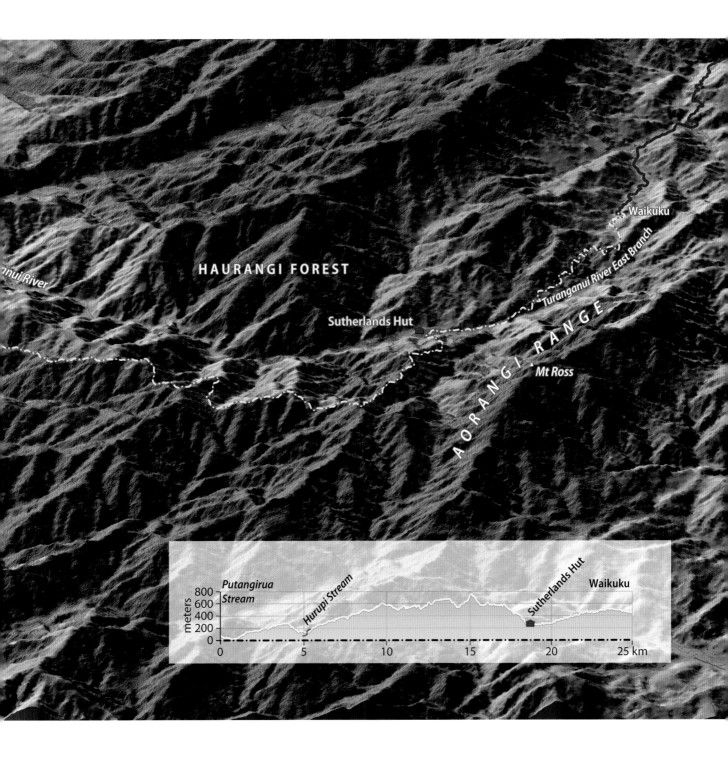

HAURANGI FOREST

Waikuku

...anui River

Turanganui River East Branch

Sutherlands Hut

A O R A N G I   R A N G E

Mt Ross

Putangirua
Stream

Hurupi Stream

Sutherlands Hut

Waikuku

meters

800
600
400
200
0

0   5   10   15   20   25 km

KARAPOTI CLASSIC
WELLINGTON

Thousands of mountain bikers have raced, ridden and pushed the Karapoti Classic's 52-kilometre course over the 25 years since its inception. Paul Kennett had a different course in mind in 1986 when the first Karapoti race took place, becoming the second mountain bike race ever held in New Zealand. For many racers, the challenge is to beat last year's time, or better still, to go under three hours. Track conditions play a big part—dry and fast one year, wet and boggy the next; but it's always a challenge. The route ridden today is little different to those early races, and makes a great recreational ride, especially going clockwise, in the opposite direction to the race.

From Birchville, at the north end of Upper Hutt, the Akatarawa Road winds above the Akatarawa River, flanked on both sides by pockets of bush and large forestry blocks. A few kilometres up and just below the Karapoti Road turn-off, a large picnic area provides an ideal spot to start from. You can choose the ford or take the bridge over the Akatarawa River and head up into the gorge on the Karapoti Road. The bush has encroached over the years narrowing the road down to almost a single track.

From McGhies Bridge, head along the edge of the Hukinga Forest to the start of a big loop. Ford the Akatarawa River and start on the steep, open climb to the 547-metre Pram Track top, named after a famous pram that rusted away there. The ridge has recently been logged but good traction should allow you to grovel to the top. Head back into the pine forest for a cool and dark undulating section of 4WD track and the final descent to Dopers Creek. This should be negotiated with caution if wet clay is encountered.

From the creek the Big Ring Boulevard ascent can be a middle-ring cruise, with some good views from the top section of Titi Road to the summit and high point at 613 metres. Native bush is regenerating here, with plenty of rain and sunshine to encourage it. The Devil's Staircase soon appears, but travelling in this direction you can ride down its spine instead of shouldering your bike up. The clay surface may look dodgy at first, but the centre ridge between the ruts provides good traction most of the time. About halfway down an old mud-encrusted motorcycle is rotting at the track edge and no doubt has an intriguing story to tell. The bottom section is often drier, but steeper, with a hairy rocky exit to a short section of bog, then a gnarly river crossing just before the Rock Garden uphill.

The Rock Garden has some handy sneak tracks bypassing the big drop-offs, with only a few short push sections required. The climb up to Deadwood is more of a challenge, with a loose and slippery slick clay surface. A gnarly descent into Cedholm Creek follows, with waving toetoe lining the banks as you ride the watery bed to the boulder-strewn and thankfully short unrideable exit. This ascends the backside of the race's first climb, through a nice bit of beech forest to a short summit. It's all downhill from there as the track winds its way high above the Akatarawa River West, eventually closing the loop.

It can be a fast ride back down the gorge with gravity on your side, but beware of other bikers and motorcycles coming your way. The final ford marks the end of a great ride.

Opposite *A blur of ferns and clay down to Dopers Creek*

Descending the Devil's Staircase in style

Map: BP32 Paraparaumu
Distance: 52 km loop
Climbing: 1600 metres
Grade: 3, but jumps up a grade in the wet
Notes: Check out www.karapoti.co.nz for the course map, race results and history.

Devil's Staircase

Deadwood Stream

to
Waikanae

HUKINGA FOREST

Akatarawa River West

Dopers Creek

Akatarawa River

Akatarawa Road

Akatarawa River West

Karapoti Road

to
Upper Hutt

Devil's
Staircase

Karapoti Road

Akatarawa River West

25   30   35   40   45   52 km

LAKE KOHANGATERA AND LAKE KOHANGA-PIRIPIRI TRACKS
WELLINGTON

The Parangarahu Lakes Area of Wellington's East Harbour Regional Park, which includes the twin lighthouses at Pencarrow Head, has a fascinating history. Maori occupied areas around both lakes and along the coast, and used inland routes through to the Wairarapa. European settlers also used these routes when they arrived in the mid 1800s. Shipwrecks were common along this busy coast, which initiated the construction of New Zealand's first permanent lighthouse. The lighthouse was completed in 1859 and was run by Mary Jane Bennett, the only woman to be appointed a lighthouse keeper in New Zealand. Such were the dangers posed by sailing into Wellington Harbour that a second lighthouse was built below the first in 1906, and in 1935 yet another was added further south at Baring Head. The last shipwreck was in 1981, with 20 previous shipwrecks well documented.

From Wellington, head to Eastbourne and down to the car-park and picnic spot just before Burdans Gate. Pedal south along the coast on the wide gravel road that runs between the sea and the hillside. Bright white sheep are dotted among the gorse, manuka, ngaio and native scrub that climbs the steep inland hill country. Driftwood, seaweed, flotsam and jetsam are strewn across the stony beaches, with rocky outcrops appearing to float out into the salt water. This is a bracing 6-kilometre warm-up ride in the salt air before attacking the steep and rewarding climbs in the Lakes Block.

As you approach Pencarrow Head the lighthouses come into view, modernised with an array of photovoltaic panels like retro Russian rockets heading for the space station. Continue past them to Fitzroy Bay, ignoring all inland side tracks. Just beyond the outlet of Lake Kohangapiripiri take the Kohangapiripiri Track and climb steeply from the lake edge to the top of the ridge. The track straddles the top of the ridge between the two lakes before racing headlong back down to the coast. Cross the second lake outlet and turn left.

The grassy Kohangatera Track is signposted and heads along the outflow and eastern side of Lake Kohangatera. This is still a working farm but stream catchments and large areas of the farm are covered in native bush or regenerating. The shallow lake edge is a mat of reeds and grasses, filled with frogs and insects. Below Finger Hill a chimney is

Stunning views out to Baring Head from Lake Kohangapiripiri ridge track

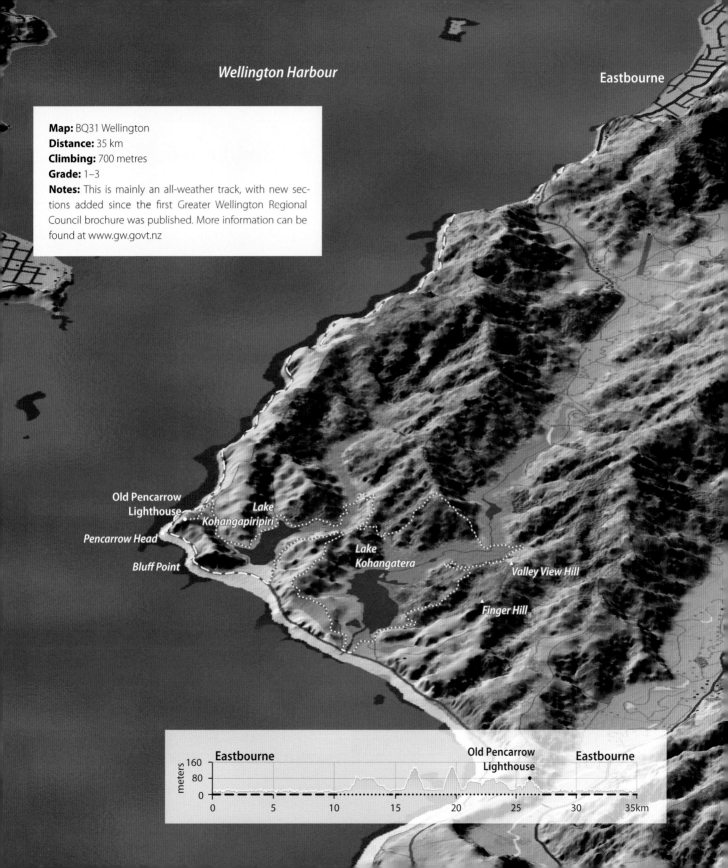

Wellington Harbour

Eastbourne

Map: BQ31 Wellington
Distance: 35 km
Climbing: 700 metres
Grade: 1–3
Notes: This is mainly an all-weather track, with new sections added since the first Greater Wellington Regional Council brochure was published. More information can be found at www.gw.govt.nz

Old Pencarrow
Lighthouse

*Lake
Kohangapiripiri*

Pencarrow Head

*Lake
Kohangatera*

Bluff Point

Valley View Hill

Finger Hill

Eastbourne

Old Pencarrow
Lighthouse

Eastbourne

meters

160

80

0   5   10   15   20   25   30   35km

The old Pencarrow Lighthouse, built below the fog line

all that remains of an old farm hut near the track. There is a Lookout Track that climbs the ridge adjacent to Valley View Hill—a short, sharp climb that leaves the legs and lungs shattered, but the views are worth every breath. From the top Wellington Harbour appears as a wide, blue mouth between the heads, with the South Island visible across Cook Strait.

At the back end of the lake, the Gollans Stream Wetland teems with birdlife, with just a narrow ribbon of water meandering through the centre of the catchment. Lush bush that has escaped earlier farm burnoffs and clearing is thriving. A boardwalk crosses its far end and the track climbs steeply up to the Lake Kohangatera lookout at 145 metres. From there it traverses to a Y intersection on the ridge top, where you head right and drop down Camerons Track to the edge of Lake Kohangapiripiri. The track branches again and you continue right onto the Kohangapiripiri Track and head up the lake to the Cameron Creek Wetland.

Cross a second boardwalk and continue around the lake to the Lighthouse Track intersection. Turn off to the right and climb up to the Old Pencarrow Lighthouse to enjoy the stunning 360-degree view—there are excellent interpretation panels along the way that give you a chance for a breather. Bluff Point lookout is only a stone's throw away, and the cliffs plummet down to the rugged coast, with views of Wellington across the water. Exit north across a stile and down a loose snatch of single track for the ride back up the coast. It may not be technical single track, but it's a great ride with stunning views.

OLD COAST ROAD
WELLINGTON

Drive south from Wainuiomata on Coast Road, which heads south through Khyber Pass to the coast. A little further on there is a large parking area by the seaside—a perfect spot from which to start the ride. Pedal east and cross the bridge over the Orongorongo River to the DOC access sign. The historic Orongorongo Station dates back to the early 1800s and is one of the few original farms still working today. After transferring your bike across the barrier to the access easement, follow the fenceline track to the boundary of the Turakirae Head Scientific Reserve. The scientific reserve is internationally renowned, providing a 7000-year geological record of earthquake upheavals in the form of five raised beaches. Maori lived in the area as far back as the moa-hunting era, and from the mid 1800s it became a major route for farmers and traders between Wellington and the Wairarapa. This is a particularly rugged piece of coastline that has claimed the lives of many sailors through shipwrecks on its rocky beaches.

Ride through the reserve on a stony 4WD track before turning inland to pick up the Old Coast Road. This hugs the base of the southern tip of the scrub-clad Rimutaka Range. From Waimarara Peak, streams feed a large semi-wetland that runs for 2 kilometres up the coast. It is home to flax and toetoe with a surprising amount of birdlife. The panoramic view extends east across Palliser Bay and out to sea, and west to the Inland and Seaward Kaikoura ranges which stretch down the east coast of the South Island. The track then climbs gradually above a row of hidden bluffs from Barney's Whare ford, eventually reaching a wide shingle and boulder fan on the Kotumu Stream. You can usually find a marked route to follow, taking the line of least resistance as it crosses to the far side. It provides a challenging piece of riding for those resistant to pushing and carrying their bikes.

Steep bush-clad slopes scarred by numerous slips now climb to the main ridge as you ride below the bluff above Fishermans Rock and onto Windy Point. Negotiate your way through the large metal gate and attempt to ride the soft sand around to the Mukamukaiti Stream ford. The bay is wide and open with a long line of wind-blown manuka running along the base of the hills and clear grassy flats that provide grazing for sheep and wild goats. A second ford marks the exit from the bay and you soon climb steeply to avoid the sea's relentless erosion of the coast and the tracks that once followed it. This is just a short undulating section, with the odd sand trap thrown in, before the terrain starts to ease off as you head to the bach settlement near the

The Old Coast Road winding its way from Windy Point

road end. These cute and inviting dwellings are perfect examples of the traditional kiwi holiday home. There is a DOC camping spot among the manuka, with a shelter, table and toilets, making it a great spot for lunch before the return journey back along the Old Coast Road.

Fording Mukamukaiti Stream below the wild Rimutaka Ranges

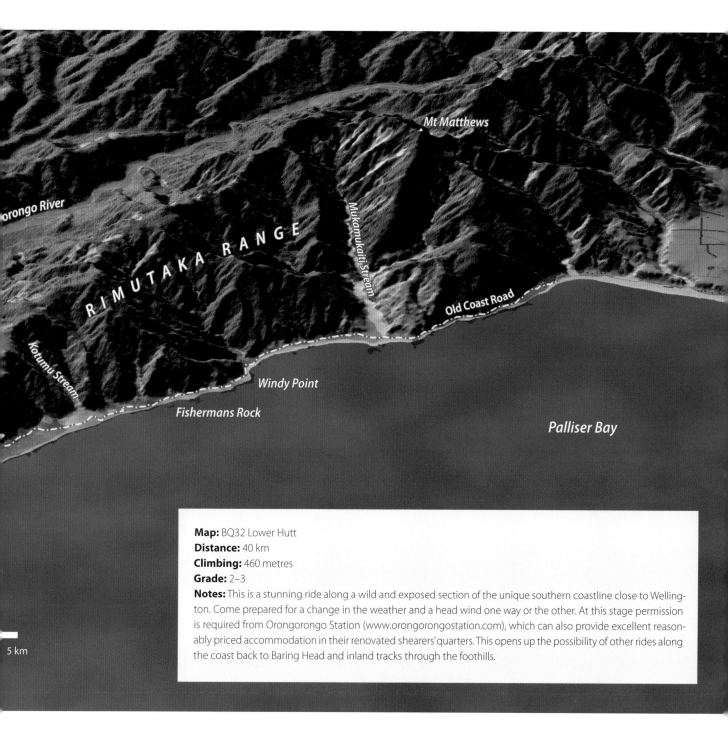

Map: BQ32 Lower Hutt
Distance: 40 km
Climbing: 460 metres
Grade: 2–3
Notes: This is a stunning ride along a wild and exposed section of the unique southern coastline close to Wellington. Come prepared for a change in the weather and a head wind one way or the other. At this stage permission is required from Orongorongo Station (www.orongorongostation.com), which can also provide excellent reasonably priced accommodation in their renovated shearers' quarters. This opens up the possibility of other rides along the coast back to Baring Head and inland tracks through the foothills.

PUKE ARIKI TRACK
WELLINGTON

Before Europeans arrived in the mid 1800s, much of the hill country between Porirua and the Hutt Valley was covered in broadleaf and podocarp forest, with rimu and rata towering over the shorter tawa and hinau trees. Maori crossed the area to travel from the Hutt Valley to the east coast, before early settlers cleared the land for farming. An old coach road crossing the Belmont Ridge was used until the late 1880s, when it was replaced by the Hayward Hills route.

The damming of the Korokoro Stream to secure a water supply for Petone led to the first purchase of reserve land in 1903. During World War II the military requisitioned over 1000 acres and built 62 concrete bunkers along the central ridge top to hold ammunition for the Pacific campaign. By the 1970s, the need to provide recreation land for a growing region saw many more blocks added, and by 1989 the 3691-hectare Belmont Regional Park had become established.

The Puke Ariki Track runs from the far northeast end of the park to its southwest corner, taking in all the park's historic sites and delivering unparalleled views and a wide variety of mountain bike terrain. The track starts from the Dry Creek carpark adjacent to State Highway 2 heading towards Upper Hutt from Wellington. A large map board and information panel shows the start of the track and the lay of the land. Climb steeply on a short piece of single track to the farm road above and follow the orange Puke Ariki markers to climb the long ridge above the Dry Creek catchments. There are some steep granny-gear rises on the last pitch to the 442-metre Boulder Hill while traversing open farm country. Ignore the Dry Creek traverse side track, but save it for another day as it's a great loop.

From Boulder Hill, named for the Stonehenge-like array of unusually shaped boulders, there is a 360-degree view of the city, the east and west coasts and across to the hazy South Island. The following downhill is fast and smooth as it heads through a low saddle, then you climb one of the main farm tracks to the first of the World War II concrete bunkers. The salt sea air and fierce southerly storms have rusted their metal attachments and the flat concrete roofs are covered with colourful lichen. It is hard to grasp the amount of work required to build these concrete monoliths as you ride towards the gas pipeline control station, which utilises one of the bunkers, and onto the airstrip. You encounter more and more of the bunkers, which seem to be around every corner, filling the gullies and littering the hillsides.

Cross the airstrip and climb steeply on a rough farm track to Round Knob, where you traverse along the narrow ridge top to Cannons Head. Ignore Middle Ridge Track as you climb again on single track to the Belmont Trig, at 456 metres the highest point of the ride. The views are outstanding and you are surrounded by stunted native trees. This is a

Riding single track amongst the regenerating bush

Climbing to Belmont Trig with a Wellington Harbour backdrop

great spot for lunch before tackling the gnarly single track downhill ahead. It's a fantastic ride down to Baked Beans Corner, with the lower section passing through an envelope of lush green bush.

From Baked Beans Corner the track drops to ford the Korokoro Stream, sidling along both banks with some gnarly technical riding. Tall pine and macrocarpa trees spear the sky above, branchless to their upper canopy. The track eventually mellows out and follows the old cast iron pipe-

line on a smooth, flowing bench above the water. This section is great riding all the way down to Cornish Street and the track end, which comes too soon. Cross State Highway 2 and head to the Petone foreshore for an ice cream, and pick up the Hutt River Trail to warm down by pedalling back to the start. The other option is to climb back up to Boulder Hill via one of the other park tracks and descend back to the start on the Dry Creek Loop track.

Baked Beans Bend, a favourite on toast

Map: BQ32 Lower Hutt
Distance: River Trail 35 km, Boulder Hill 50 km
Climbing: River Trail 1050 metres, Boulder Hill 2150 metres
Grade: 3+
Notes: The Belmont Regional Park brochure has an excellent map and additional information about the park. Camping is available at the Stratton Street valley and at Dry Creek, contact belmontranger@gw.govt.nz to book. Pick a fine day with little wind.

Round Knob

Boulder Hill

Dry Creek

to
Upper Hutt

annons Head

BELMONT REGIONAL PARK

2

Hutt River

Lower Hutt

ne

meters

500

250

0

Dry Creek

Boulder Hill

Round Knob

Belmont

Korokoro Stream

Boulder Hill

Dry Creek

0   5   10   15   20   25   30   35   40   45   48 km

RIMUTAKA INCLINE
WELLINGTON

The 22,000 hectares of Rimutaka Forest Park cover much of the Rimutaka Range and provide an easily accessible recreation area for the people of greater Wellington. Among its mountain biking attractions is the historic Rimutaka Incline. A railway line had been constructed from Wellington to Upper Hutt by 1874, but crossing the Rimutaka Range into the Wairarapa presented a major challenge as the gradients on the eastern side were too steep for a conventional railway. The solution for those sections of line was a newly invented system that gripped an additional centre track, designed by John Fell for use in the French mountains.

Orders were duly placed for four of these new engines, and construction of the track for them to run on was well under way by 1876. The first 8000-part kitset engine arrived in 1877 and was immediately put to use to assist construction of the line. The line was opened in 1878, but it proved costly to maintain, and was prone to slips and tree falls due to the heavy rain and high winds the Rimutaka Range often experiences. In fact, in 1880 a huge gust on an exposed corner nicknamed Siberia blew two carriages and a brake van off the rails and down the hillside, killing three passengers.

Eventually the high cost of maintenance and the desire for a faster, safer route saw the construction of a new line, which included an 8.8-kilometre tunnel, the longest in New Zealand, under the Rimutaka Range. The new route bypassed the incline completely, and in 1955, after 77 years of service, that section of line was closed down. The Rimutaka Rail Trail came into being during the 1980s, following the original railway line and providing an alternative historic route to Featherston and the Wairarapa. To get there, head 9 kilometres north from Upper Hutt and turn right in Kaitoke onto the Pakuratahi Forest Road. Head to the road end carpark where the track starts straight ahead. Pedal the pleasant 1 in 30 grade as the track climbs adjacent to the Pakuratahi River and through an old pine plantation. As the track turns east you pass above the Rimutaka rail tunnel, crossing the river soon after.

There are restored rail bridges and interpretation panels alongside the track, which bring the history of steam and steel to life. The 400-metre summit is soon reached and is the start of the track's longest tunnel, which is very dark on an overcast day, so it is best to take a torch. The descent is twice as steep as the climb, but is still gradual in mountain bike terms. It traverses high above Cross Creek, sidling around the ridge before heading due east to Cross Creek Station. The native bush is slowly returning in places where it was once completely cleared, often as a result of sparks from the steam engines starting fires. Just after the second tunnel a large slip appears in Horseshoe Gully from just below Deraa Peak. The stream washed out the curved earth embankment in 1967, and presents a steep descent with an alluvial gravel ford to be crossed. A third tunnel completes the set, dug through difficult country on steep terrain.

The bottom of the line is the site of old railway yards that were once part of the Cross Creek Station and settlement, one of the most remote postings railway staff could be sent to. Take the Cross Creek single track on your right, which winds through tall manuka and broadleaves on the true right of Cross Creek to the Cross Creek Road carpark. Head out to Featherston for an ice cream or lunch before reversing the ride.

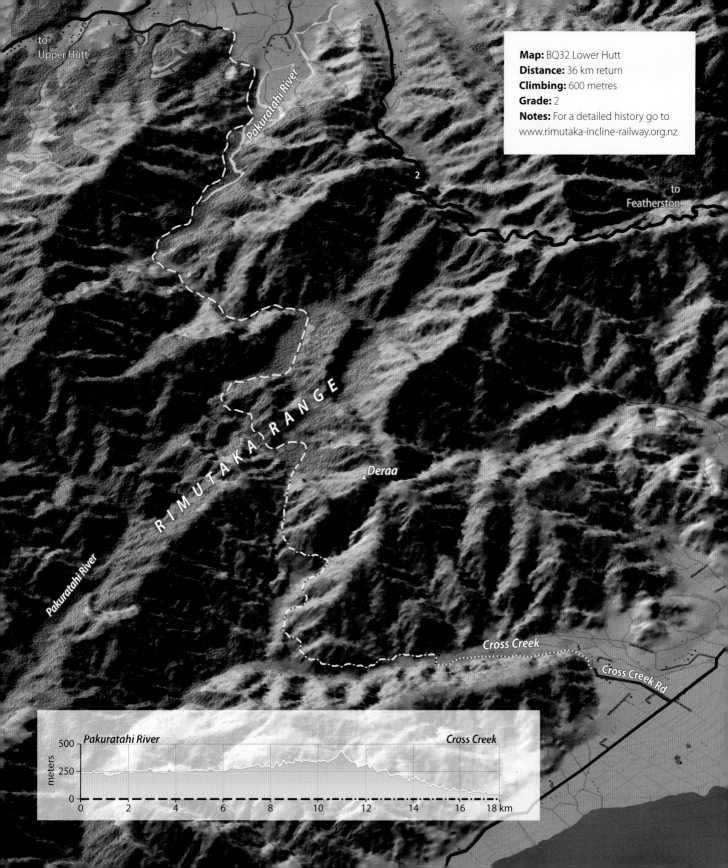

to
Upper Hutt

Pakuratahi River

Map: BQ32 Lower Hutt
Distance: 36 km return
Climbing: 600 metres
Grade: 2
Notes: For a detailed history go to
www.rimutaka-incline-railway.org.nz

2

to
Featherston

R I M U T A K A   R A N G E

Deraa

Pakuratahi River

Cross Creek

Cross Creek Rd

500

meters

250

Pakuratahi River

Cross Creek

0

0   2   4   6   8   10   12   14   16   18 km

Steam boilers, just below the track summit and tunnel

SKYLINE TRACK–RED ROCKS
WELLINGTON

The Skyline Track follows the hilltops above Wellington from Johnsonville's Kaukau Peak to Sinclair Head and the Red Rocks at the southern tip of the city. On a fine day with little or no wind it is one of the best ridge-top point-to-point rides in New Zealand. The track has been a long-time favourite of the walking fraternity, and is now included as part of the Te Araroa Trail, a walking trail covering the length of the country.

The track starts from a small reserve at the end of Carmichael Street in the quiet suburb of Johnsonville. Pedal through the reserve and up a gentle climb on the Old Coach Road. After a few hundred metres hang a left onto a poled route to enjoy a brutal granny-gear climb that traverses up to Kaukau Peak at 445 metres. Expansive views of the harbour and the city are your reward at the top. A large map board lays out the track ahead, judiciously marked as both Skyline Track and Te Araroa Trail, along with the rest of the local network that radiates down to the city and suburbs.

Follow the yellow reflector-topped markers and descend the southwest ridge through open farmland and short native scrub. This is a varied ride on a mix of single track, stock track and farm track, with some technical climbs and traverses thrown in. The rows of wind turbines slowly turning on Wellington's western hills are a good indicator of riding conditions to come as you pass them all the way to Makara Hill. Purpose-built single track winds around the edge of one of the highest sections of Karori before switchbacking down to a block of tall pine trees, through which you can travel fast to the sealed Makara Road.

Turn right and head a short distance to the Makara Hill mountain bike sign. Go past the large metal gate and climb steeply to the water tank above, where a trail map is situated beside the start of Varley's Track. Ride on and zigzag your way up to Zac's Track through short regenerating native bush. Zac's Track takes you all the way to the top, with excellent open views across Wellington's west coast and foothills. The top is dominated by a large transmitter tower,

with a much smaller sign pointing to great mountain bike destinations around the world.

Go straight ahead onto the Ridge Line Track for a short climb followed by an exciting descent. Continue on to either Swig or Lazy Fern Track for a rollercoaster ride all the way down to the Makara Hill carpark. There are picnic tables and green grass to have your lunch on, cool water, toilets and a bike wash if you feel like sprucing up your mount for the next phase of the ride. Many kilometres of magic single track flow around this peak and are being constantly added to. Re-fuel and pedal right onto seal, then after a few hundred metres turn left up Hazelwood Ave and right onto Fitzgerald Ave. Follow this to a green space at the bush edge where there is a large map board.

Take the Salvation single track and climb the northern ridge of Wrights Hill almost to the top. Dappled light filters down through the native bush, and thick leaf litter blankets much of the ground. This is an honest climb that takes you to a sealed road where you head right for a short distance then left onto John's Track. This is a superb section of single track that climbs almost to the top of the hill, where the World War II bunkers and parade ground are situated. Don't go there, but follow the arrows up the Lookout Track to the Karori Sanctuary fence line.

Head right and follow the track along the fence line, which is an expensive marvel of predator-proof engineering. This is an undulating dirt track that climbs more than it descends and steepens up markedly near the top, just when the legs are needing a rest. You pop out of the bush onto a single-lane tarseal road, where you turn right and

Above *Halfway to Red Rocks and the centre of mountain biking*
Following page *Red Rocks below, with a hazy South Island on the horizon*

climb towards the 495-metre Hawkins Hill, with its golf ball and mysterious castle perched in the clouds. Once past the castle the start of the Red Rocks downhill is on your left. On the east side of the ridge a new section of single track winds from the reserve to join the downhill you are about to embark upon.

Head around the locked gate and down this lumpy track for a few hundred metres, then take the first side track on your right. This climbs initially before following the ridge between coastal shrubs, with stunning views across the rugged southern coast below. About halfway down a narrow ridge-line track descends steeply before peeling off to the west over large boulders and scree, with an exceptionally steep and loose section that slides down to the creek at the bottom. As an option about halfway down the preceding section, a new piece of single track leads into the stream gully for a technical blast down to the coast.

The coastal track heads east on sand and stone, sandwiched between high cliffs, rocky outcrops and the surf pounding the beach. It passes a rustic old bach, Red Rocks and the old Owhiro Bay quarry. The tarseal begins at the Owhiro Bay carpark, where you can catch a car shuttle, or pedal into town on Happy Valley–Ohiro Road and catch the train back to Johnsonville for a short climb back to the start. This is a big day out with lots of fantastic views, single track and climbing.

Map: BQ31 Wellington
Distance: 45 km
Climbing: 1300 metres
Grade: 3–4
Notes: Hopeless in a strong wind and hard work in the wet, but there are plenty of side tracks you can bail on.

Johnsonville

Kaukau

Makara Peak

Wrights Hill

Karori Sanctuary

Wellington

Happy Valley

Hawkins Hill

Red Rocks

Sinclair Head

meters

500

250

0

Johnsonville

Kaukau

Makara Peak

Wrights Hill

Hawkins Hill

Red Rocks

0   5   10   15   20   25   30   35   40   45 km

CAPE PALLISER TRACK
WAIRARAPA

Exposed at the southern tip of the North Island, the coastline around Cape Palliser is windswept and rugged, washed by the bright blue (on a clear day) waters of the Pacific Ocean. The prevailing current moves tonnes of round, grey rocks along the coast to form a steep, stony beach. Above the beach a thin strip of coastal grasses and tussock stretches to the clay hills that rise abruptly along much of the coast, and are often eroded into spectacular clay formations. Manuka has colonised much of the area, with a variety of coastal natives growing further inland.

From the DOC campground at Putangirua Stream, head south down the coast on Whatarangi Road. This follows the coastline, alternating between smooth gravel and sections of tarseal laid in the middle of nowhere. Travel around the edge of Palliser Bay to the small fishing village of Ngawi, with its beach parking lot full of brightly painted bulldozers and a cluster of traditional kiwi baches below the scrub-covered hills. It's an amazing first sight, these ancient earthmovers long past their prime, put out to pasture in a retirement home by the sea. The sight of one of these old machines dragging a huge fishing boat full of fish and nets through the pounding surf and up onto the beach makes you feel like clapping. This is a good place to ride from.

Saddle up and pedal around the coast past Te Kawakawa Rocks for your first view of Cape Palliser lighthouse. Cape Palliser often bears the brunt of the Cook Strait gales, making this one of the windiest parts of an extremely exposed coast. An adjacent fence running along the road has had most of its galvanising sandblasted away from the wire, and the supporting fence posts have a distinctive sandblasted grain. Numerous ships have been wrecked in the area, so a lighthouse was proposed and first lit in 1897. It was built on a ledge 78 metres up a bluff, so oil and kerosene had to be hauled up using only a hand winch before an electric lamp was installed. The keepers' houses were built below at sea level, with 258 wooden steps climbing steeply to the base of the lighthouse.

A 4WD track starts from here and heads through Aorangi Forest Park and along the more southerly facing aspect of the coast. The Polynesian navigator Kupe lived in this area, known as Matakitaki, and his sacred pool can be found in a reserve near the lighthouse. The area was gazetted as a forest park in 1978 and stock was progressively removed and exotic species planted to control erosion.

From the hills, matagouri, divaricating shrubs, manuka and cabbage trees grow all the way to the rocky outcrops near the sea. The riding changes character here, climbing and descending in stream gullies and through rock-strewn terraces. Ford the Waitetuna Stream. A swimming hole exists where the stream exits the hills above; a place to visit on the way back. A couple of kilometres of open grassland flow into a forest of tall manuka, contrasting markedly with the bright green undergrowth and providing shade for a snack at the edge of the forest.

Beyond here, a huge shingle fan descends from Mataopera Stream and Raeotutemahuta Peak to the water's edge. Soft wheel tracks ascend this massive scree slide that soon becomes unrideable. Clear of the scree, the track heads vaguely northeast on a loose and rocky surface. The final climb provides a view along the east coast to White Rock and Te Kaukau Point. The wide bay and its reef provide a fine surf spot when the tides are right.

After a final descent through cabbage trees, the track levels out and wanders to Ngapotiki, where it meets the formed road. Ngapotiki has a large grassy camping area

Returning from the Waitetuna Stream swimming hole after a cool dip

for tents and is characterised by windswept cabbage trees straight out of a Dr Seuss book. It's a good place to have lunch and enjoy the view and warm sun before your return.

A 145-kilometre, two-day round trip from Martinborough is possible, taking in many of the scenic back roads. The track would certainly be suitable for panniers and the ride provides a great way to see this wild and woolly part of the North Island's southern coastline and inland foothills.

Heading to the massive shingle fan at the north end of the ride

Map: BR33 Ngawi
Distance: 38 km return
Grade: 2
Notes: 35 km south of Martinborough, before Lake Ferry, turn left onto Whangaimoana Road, which continues to the Putangirua DOC campsite. There is also a good camping ground at Lake Ferry and a hotel that offers meals and accommodation.

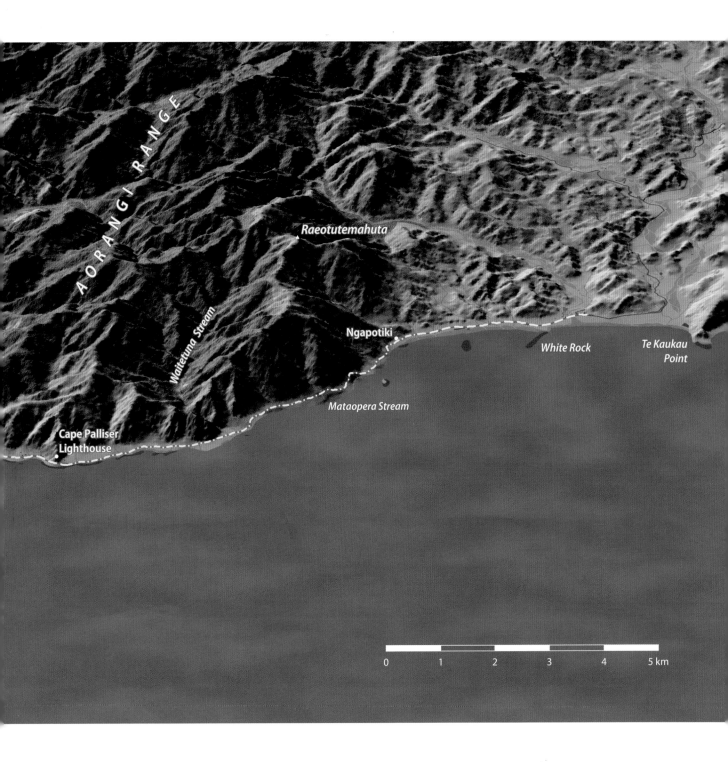

AORANGI RANGE

Raeotutemahuta

Waitetuna Stream

Ngapotiki

White Rock

Te Kaukau Point

Mataopera Stream

Cape Palliser Lighthouse

0 1 2 3 4 5 km

OTHER BOOKS BY CRAIG POTTON PUBLISHING

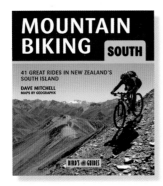

Mountain Biking South
DAVE MITCHELL
$39.99 © 2010
ISBN 978 1 877517 32 7

Tramping in New Zealand
SHAUN BARNETT & GEOGRAPHX
$39.99 © 2006
ISBN 978 1 877333 51 4

Day Walks in New Zealand
SHAUN BARNETT & GEOGRAPHX
$39.99 © 2007
ISBN 978 1 877333 67 5

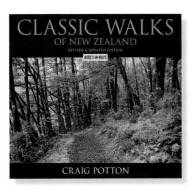

Classic Walks of New Zealand
CRAIG POTTON
$39.99 © 2009
ISBN 978 1 877517 06 8

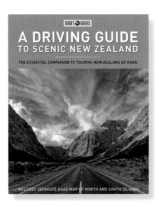

A Driving Guide to Scenic New Zealand
$39.99 © 2008
ISBN 978 1 877333 94 1

Classic Tramping of New Zealand
CRAIG POTTON
$39.99 © 2010
ISBN 978 1 877517 24 2

North Island Weekend Tramps
SHAUN BARNETT
$39.99 © 2008
ISBN 978 1 877333 95 8

The New Zealand Tramper's Handbook
SARAH BENNET & LEE SLATER
$24.99 © 2010
ISBN 978 1 877517 29 7

South Island Weekend Tramps
NICK GROVES
$39.99 © 2008
ISBN 978 1 877333 96 5